Clymer Motorcycle Repair Series

HONDA

250 & 350cc TWINS • 1964-1974
SERVICE • REPAIR • MAINTENANCE

CANCEl

CLYMER PUBLICATIONS

The world's finest publisher of mechanical how-to manuals
INTERTEC PUBLISHING CORPORATION
P.O. Box 12901, Overland Park, Kansas 66282-2901

Copyright ©1983 Intertec Publishing Corporation

FIRST EDITION
First Printing April, 1978
Second Printing July, 1978
Third Printing April, 1979
Fourth Printing September, 1979

SECOND EDITION
Revised by Ed Scott
First Printing December, 1980
Second Printing July, 1982

THIRD EDITION
Revised by Ed Scott
First Printing October, 1983
Second Printing November, 1984
Third Printing October, 1985
Fourth Printing January, 1987
Fifth Printing October, 1988
Sixth Printing April, 1990
Seventh Printing December, 1991
Eighth Printing September, 1993

Printed in U.S.A.

ISBN: 0-89287-209-8

MOTORCYCLE INDUSTRY COUNCIL

INTERTEC PUBLISHING CORP.

President and CEO   Raymond E. Maloney

Group Vice President   Bill J. Wiesner

EDITORIAL

Editorial Director
Randy Stephens

Editors
Mike Hall
Mark Jacobs

Technical Writers
Robert Mills
Ron Wright
Ed Scott
Michael Morlan

Inventory/Production Manager
Terry Distin

Lead Editorial Assistant
Elizabeth Couzens

Editorial Assistants
Shirley Renicker
Jon Worley

Technical Illustrators
Steve Amos
Robert Caldwell
Mitzi McCarthy
Diana Kirkland

MARKETING

Marketing Director
Chris Charlton

Advertising and Promotions Manager
Katherine Nelms

Advertising Assistant
Wendy Blumenthal

Graphic Designer
Anita Blattner

SALES AND ADMINISTRATION

Director of Sales
Dutch Sadler

Accounts Manager
Ted Metzger

Sales Coordinator
Lynn Reynolds

Customer Service and Administration Manager
Joan Jackson

The following books and guides are published by Intertec Publishing Corp.

CLYMER SHOP MANUALS
Boat Motors and Drives
Motorcycles and ATVs
Snowmobiles
Personal Watercraft

ABOS/INTERTEC BLUE BOOKS AND TRADE-IN GUIDES
Recreational Vehicles
Outdoor Power Equipment
Agricultural Tractors
Lawn and Garden Tractors
Motorcycles and ATVs
Snowmobiles
Boats and Motors
Personal Watercraft

AIRCRAFT BLUEBOOK-PRICE DIGEST
Airplanes
Helicopters

I&T SHOP MANUALS
Tractors

INTERTEC SERVICE MANUALS
Snowmobiles
Outdoor Power Equipment
Personal Watercraft
Gasoline and Diesel Engines
Recreational Vehicles
Boat Motors and Drives
Motorcycles
Lawn and Garden Tractor

HONDA

250 & 350cc TWINS • 1964-1974

SERVICE • REPAIR • MAINTENANCE

CONTENTS

QUICK REFERENCE DATA

IGNITION TIMING

The "LF" mark on the alternator rotor must align with the index pointer just as the left-hand ignition breaker points begin to open. The right-hand ignition breaker points should just begin to open as the "F" mark and index pointer align.

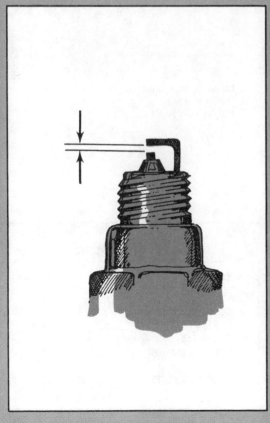

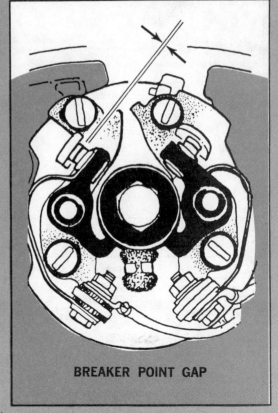

BREAKER POINT GAP

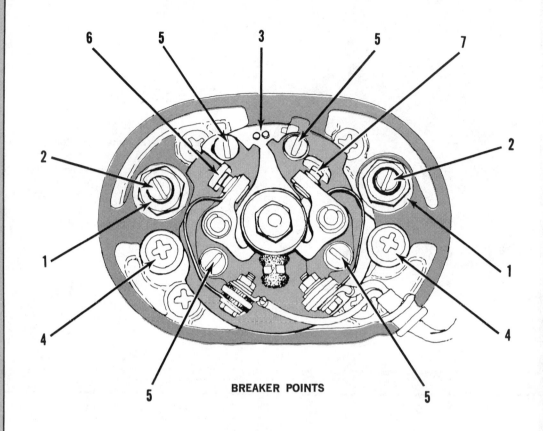

BREAKER POINTS

1. Locknut
2. Adjuster
3. Pry slots
4. Base plate retaining screws

5. Breaker points retaining screws
6. Left cylinder points
7. Right cylinder points

TUNE-UP SPECIFICATIONS

	Inches	Millimeters
Breaker point gap	0.012-0.016	0.3-0.4
Spark plug gap	0.028-0.032	0.7-0.8
Valve clearance		
250		
Intake	0.002	0.05
Exhaust	0.003	0.08
350		
Intake	0.002	0.05
Exhaust	0.004	0.10

CARBURETOR FLOAT HEIGHT

Model	Inches	Millimeters
250	0.75	19.0
CB350, CL350		
Prior to engine No. 1045165	0.75	19.0
Engine No. 1045165-1065278	0.83	21.0
Engine No. 1065279	1.02	26.0
SL350	0.98	25.0

DRIVE CHAIN ADJUSTMENT

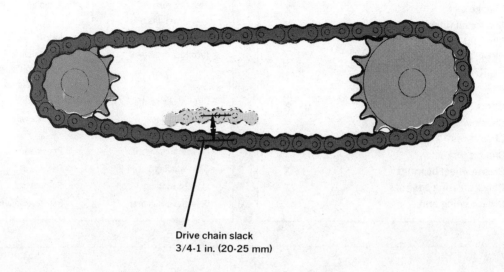

Drive chain slack
3/4-1 in. (20-25 mm)

TIRES

Tire Size	Inflation Pressure (psi)
2.50-18	23
2.75-18	23
3.00-18	23
3.25-18	23
3.50-18	23
4.00-18	23
3.00-19	23
3.25-19	23

FORK OIL CAPACITY
(AFTER DISASSEMBLY)

Model	Ounces	Cubic Centimeters
CB & CL250, 350 CB & CL250, 350K1. K2. K3	6.6-6.9	195-205
CB250, 350K4. CL350K4. CB350G, CL350K5	4.2-4.4	125-130
SL350. SL350K1. SL350K2	6.1-6.4	180-190

ENGINE OIL QUANTITY

Model	Pints	Liters
250	3.2	1.5
350	4.2	2.0

ADJUSTMENTS

Adjustment	Measurement
Drive chain play	3/4-1 in. (20-25mm)
Front brake lever free play	3/16-5/16 in. (5-8mm)
Rear brake pedal free play	3/4-1 in. (20-25mm)
Clutch lever free play	3/4 in. (20mm)

ENGINE OIL GRADE

Temperature Range	Oil Viscosity
Below 32°F	10W, 10W-30, or 10W-40
32 to 60°F	20W, 10W-30, or 10W-40
Above 60°F	30W, 10W-30, or 10W-40

MAINTENANCE SCHEDULE

Maintenance Item	Miles		
	1,000	3,000	6,000
Engine tune-up		X	
Check battery	X		
Change oil	X	X	X
Service oil filter			X
Adjust clutch		X	
Check lights and horn	X		
Adjust chain	X		
Adjust brakes	X		
Check brake lining			X
Check wheels	X		
Check tires	X		
Change fork oil		X	
Grease wheel bearings			X
Check steering bearings			X
Grease swing arm		X	

IGNITION – NO SPARK/WEAK SPARK

Probable Cause	Remedy
• Discharged battery	Charge battery
• Defective fuse	Replace
• Defective main switch	Replace
• Loose or corroded connections	Clean and tighten
• Broken wire	Repair
• Incorrect point gap	Reset points. Be sure to readjust ignition timing
• Dirty or oily points	Clean points
• Spark plug lead damaged	Replace wire
• Broken primary wire	Repair wire
• Open winding in coil	Replace coil
• Shorted winding in coil	Replace coil
• Defective condenser	Replace condenser

— NOTES —

HONDA

250 & 350cc TWINS · 1964-1974

SERVICE · REPAIR · MAINTENANCE

INTRODUCTION

This detailed, comprehensive manual covers the 1964-1974 250 and 350cc Honda Twins models. The expert text gives complete information on maintenance, repair, and overhaul. Hundreds of photos and drawings guide you through every step. The book includes all you need to know to keep your Honda running right.

Where repairs are practical for the owner/mechanic, complete procedures are given. Equally important, difficult jobs are pointed out. Such operations are usually more economically performed by a dealer or independent garage.

A shop manual is a reference. You want to be able to find information fast. As in all Clymer books, this one is designed with this in mind. All chapters are thumb tabbed. Important items are indexed at the rear of the book. Finally, all the most frequently used specifications and capacities are summarized on the *Quick Reference* pages at the front of the book.

Keep the book handy. Carry it in your tool box. It will help you to better understand your Honda, lower repair and maintenance costs, and generally improve your satisfaction with your bike.

CHAPTER ONE

GENERAL INFORMATION

The troubleshooting, maintenance, tune-up, and step-by-step repair procedures in this book are written specifically for the owner and home mechanic. The text is accompanied by helpful photos and diagrams to make the job as clear and correct as possible.

Troubleshooting, maintenance, tune-up, and repair are not difficult if you know what to do and what tools and equipment to use. Anyone of average intelligence, with some mechanical ability, and not afraid to get their hands dirty can perform most of the procedures in this book.

In some cases, a repair job may require tools or skills not reasonably expected of the home mechanic. These procedures are noted in each chapter and it is recommended that you take the job to your dealer, a competent mechanic, or a machine shop.

MANUAL ORGANIZATION

This chapter provides general information, safety and service hints. Also included are lists of recommended shop and emergency tools as well as a brief description of troubleshooting and tune-up equipment.

Chapter Two provides methods and suggestions for quick and accurate diagnosis and repair of problems. Troubleshooting procedures discuss typical symptoms and logical methods to pinpoint the trouble.

Chapter Three explains all periodic lubrication and routine maintenance necessary to keep your motorcycle running well. Chapter Three also includes recommended tune-up procedures, eliminating the need to constantly consult chapters on the various subassemblies.

Subsequent chapters cover specific systems such as the engine, transmission, and electrical system. Each of these chapters provides disassembly, inspection, repair, and assembly procedures in a simple step-by-step format. If a repair is impractical for the home mechanic it is indicated. In these cases it is usually faster and less expensive to have the repairs made by a dealer or competent repair shop. Essential specifications are included in the appropriate chapters.

When special tools are required to perform a task included in this manual, the tools are illustrated. It may be possible to borrow or rent these tools. The inventive mechanic may also be able to find a suitable substitute in his tool box, or to fabricate one.

The terms NOTE, CAUTION, and WARNING have specific meanings in this manual. A NOTE provides additional or explanatory information. A

CAUTION is used to emphasize areas where equipment damage could result if proper precautions are not taken. A WARNING is used to stress those areas where personal injury or death could result from negligence, in addition to possible mechanical damage.

SERVICE HINTS

Time, effort, and frustration will be saved and possible injury will be prevented if you observe the following practices.

Most of the service procedures covered are straightforward and can be performed by anyone reasonably handy with tools. It is suggested, however, that you consider your own capabilities carefully before attempting any operation involving major disassembly of the engine.

Some operations, for example, require the use of a press. It would be wiser to have these performed by a shop equipped for such work, rather than to try to do the job yourself with makeshift equipment. Other procedures require precision measurements. Unless you have the skills and equipment required, it would be better to have a qualified repair shop make the measurements for you.

Repairs go much faster and easier if the parts that will be worked on are clean before you begin. There are special cleaners for washing the engine and related parts. Brush or spray on the cleaning solution, let stand, then rinse it away with a garden hose. Clean all oily or greasy parts with cleaning solvent as you remove them.

WARNING
Never use gasoline as a cleaning agent. It presents an extreme fire hazard. Be sure to work in a well-ventilated area when using cleaning solvent. Keep a fire extinguisher, rated for gasoline fires, handy in any case.

Much of the labor charge for repairs made by dealers is for the removal and disassembly of other parts to reach the defective unit. It is frequently possible to perform the preliminary operations yourself and then take the defective unit in to the dealer for repair, at considerable savings.

Once you have decided to tackle the job yourself, make sure you locate the appropriate section in this manual, and read it entirely. Study the illustrations and text until you have a good idea of what is involved in completing the job satisfactorily. If special tools are required, make arrangements to get them before you start. Also, purchase any known defective parts prior to starting on the procedure. It is frustrating and time-consuming to get partially into a job and then be unable to complete it.

Simple wiring checks can be easily made at home, but knowledge of electronics is almost a necessity for performing tests with complicated electronic testing gear.

During disassembly of parts keep a few general cautions in mind. Force is rarely needed to get things apart. If parts are a tight fit, like a bearing in a case, there is usually a tool designed to separate them. Never use a screwdriver to pry apart parts with machined surfaces such as cylinder head or crankcase halves. You will mar the surfaces and end up with leaks.

Make diagrams wherever similar-appearing parts are found. You may think you can remember where everything came from — but mistakes are costly. There is also the possibility you may get sidetracked and not return to work for days or even weeks — in which interval, carefully laid out parts may have become disturbed.

Tag all similar internal parts for location, and mark all mating parts for position. Record number and thickness of any shims as they are removed. Small parts such as bolts can be identified by placing them in plastic sandwich bags that are sealed and labeled with masking tape.

Wiring should be tagged with masking tape and marked as each wire is removed. Again, do not rely on memory alone.

Disconnect battery ground cable before working near electrical connections and before disconnecting wires. Never run the engine with the battery disconnected; the alternator could be seriously damaged.

Protect finished surfaces from physical damage or corrosion. Keep gasoline and brake fluid off painted surfaces.

Frozen or very tight bolts and screws can often be loosened by soaking with penetrating oil like Liquid Wrench or WD-40, then sharply striking the bolt head a few times with a hammer and punch (or screwdriver for screws). Avoid heat unless absolutely necessary, since it may melt, warp, or remove the temper from many parts.

Avoid flames or sparks when working near a charging battery or flammable liquids, such as gasoline.

No parts, except those assembled with a press fit, require unusual force during assembly. If a part is hard to remove or install, find out why before proceeding.

Cover all openings after removing parts to keep dirt, small tools, etc., from falling in.

When assembling two parts, start all fasteners, then tighten evenly.

Wiring connections and brake shoes, drums, pads, and discs and contact surfaces in dry clutches should be kept clean and free of grease and oil.

When assembling parts, be sure all shims and washers are replaced exactly as they came out.

Whenever a rotating part butts against a stationary part, look for a shim or washer. Use new gaskets if there is any doubt about the condition of old ones. Generally, you should apply gasket cement to one mating surface only, so the parts may be easily disassembled in the future. A thin coat of oil on gaskets helps them seal effectively.

Heavy grease can be used to hold small parts in place if they tend to fall out during assembly. However, keep grease and oil away from electrical, clutch, and brake components.

High spots may be sanded off a piston with sandpaper, but emery cloth and oil do a much more professional job.

Carburetors are best cleaned by disassembling them and soaking the parts in a commercial carburetor cleaner. Never soak gaskets and rubber parts in these cleaners. Never use wire to clean out jets and air passages; they are easily damaged. Use compressed air to blow out the carburetor, but only if the float has been removed first.

Take your time and do the job right. Do not forget that a newly rebuilt engine must be broken in the same as a new one. Refer to your owner's manual for the proper break-in procedures.

SAFETY FIRST

Professional mechanics can work for years and never sustain a serious injury. If you observe a few rules of common sense and safety, you can enjoy many safe hours servicing your motorcycle. You could hurt yourself or damage the motorcycle if you ignore these rules.

1. Never use gasoline as a cleaning solvent.

2. Never smoke or use a torch in the vicinity of flammable liquids such as cleaning solvent in open containers.

3. Never smoke or use a torch in an area where batteries are being charged. Highly explosive hydrogen gas is formed during the charging process.

4. Use the proper sized wrenches to avoid damage to nuts and injury to yourself.

5. When loosening a tight or stuck nut, be guided by what would happen if the wrench should slip. Protect yourself accordingly.

6. Keep your work area clean and uncluttered.

7. Wear safety goggles during all operations involving drilling, grinding, or use of a cold chisel.

8. Never use worn tools.

9. Keep a fire extinguisher handy and be sure it is rated for gasoline (Class B) and electrical (Class C) fires.

EXPENDABLE SUPPLIES

Certain expendable supplies are necessary. These include grease, oil, gasket cement, wiping rags, cleaning solvent, and distilled water. Also, special locking compounds, silicone lubricants, and engine and carburetor cleaners may be useful. Cleaning solvent is available at most service stations and distilled water for the battery is available at supermarkets.

SHOP TOOLS

For complete servicing and repair you will need an assortment of ordinary hand tools (**Figure 1**).

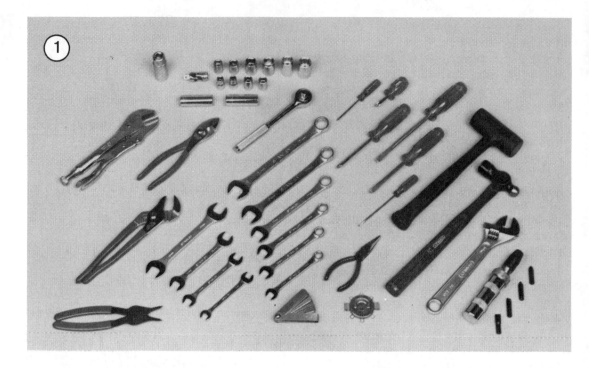

As a minimum, these include:

a. Combination wrenches
b. Sockets
c. Plastic mallet
d. Small hammer
e. Impact driver
f. Snap ring pliers
g. Gas pliers
h. Phillips screwdrivers
i. Slot (common) screwdrivers
j. Feeler gauges
k. Spark plug gauge
l. Spark plug wrench

Special tools required are shown in the chapters covering the particular repair in which they are used.

Engine tune-up and troubleshooting procedures require other special tools and equipment. These are described in detail in the following sections.

EMERGENCY TOOL KITS

Highway

A small emergency tool kit kept on the bike is handy for road emergencies which otherwise could leave you stranded. The tools and spares listed below and shown in **Figure 2** will let you handle most roadside repairs.

a. Motorcycle tool kit (original equipment)
b. Impact driver
c. Silver waterproof sealing tape (duct tape)
d. Hose-clamps (3 sizes)
e. Silicone sealer
f. Lock 'N' Seal
g. Flashlight
h. Tire patch kit
i. Tire irons
j. Plastic pint bottle (for oil)
k. Waterless hand cleaner
l. Rags for clean up

Off-Road

A few simple tools and aids carried on the motorcycle can mean the difference between walking or riding back to camp or to where repairs can be made. See **Figure 3**.

A few essential spare parts carried in your truck or van can prevent a day or weekend of trail riding from being spoiled. See **Figure 4**.

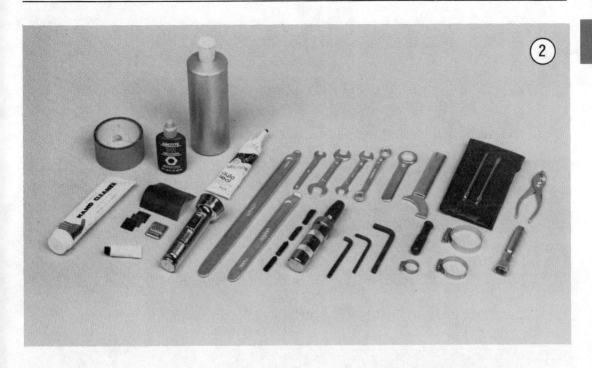

On the Motorcycle

a. Motorcycle tool kit (original equipment)
b. Drive chain master link
c. Tow line
d. Spark plug
e. Spark plug wrench
f. Shifter lever
g. Clutch/brake lever
h. Silver waterproof sealing tape (duct tape)
i. Loctite Lock 'N' Seal

In the Truck

a. Control cables (throttle, clutch, brake)
b. Silicone sealer
c. Tire patch kit
d. Tire irons
e. Tire pump
f. Impact driver
g. Oil

WARNING
Tools and spares should be carried on the motorcycle — not in clothing where a simple fall could result in serious injury from a sharp tool.

TROUBLESHOOTING AND TUNE-UP EQUIPMENT

Voltmeter, Ohmmeter, and Ammeter

For testing the ignition or electrical system, a good voltmeter is required. For motorcycle use, an instrument covering 0-20 volts is satisfactory. One which also has a 0-2 volt scale is necessary for testing relays, points, or individual contacts where voltage drops are much smaller. Accuracy should be ± ½ volt.

An ohmmeter measures electrical resistance. This instrument is useful for checking continuity (open and short circuits), and testing fuses and lights.

The ammeter measures electrical current. Ammeters for motorcycle use should cover 0-50 amperes and 0-250 amperes. These are useful for checking battery charging and starting current.

Several inexpensive VOM's (volt-ohm-milli-ammeter) combine all three instruments into one which fits easily in any tool box. See **Figure 5**. However, the ammeter ranges are usually too small for motorcycle work.

Hydrometer

The hydrometer gives a useful indication of battery condition and charge by measuring the

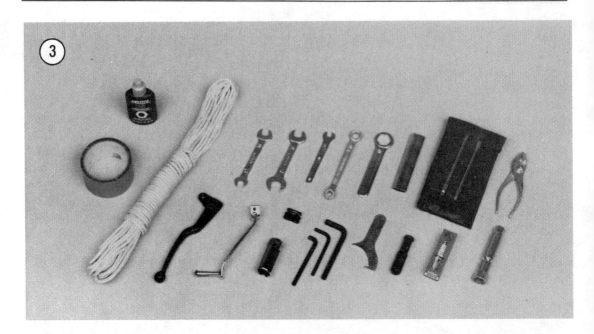

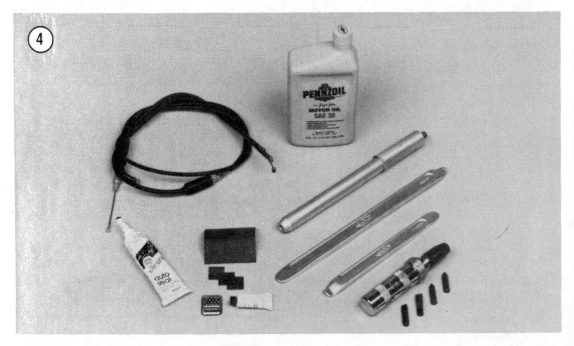

specific gravity of the electrolyte in each cell. See **Figure 6**. Complete details on use and interpretation of readings are provided in the electrical chapter.

Compression Tester

The compression tester measures the compression pressure built up in each cylinder. The results, when properly interpreted, can indicate

general cylinder, ring, and valve condition. See **Figure 7**. Extension lines are available for hard-to-reach cylinders.

Dwell Meter (Contact Breaker Point Ignition Only)

A dwell meter measures the distance in degrees of cam rotation that the breaker points remain closed while the engine is running. Since

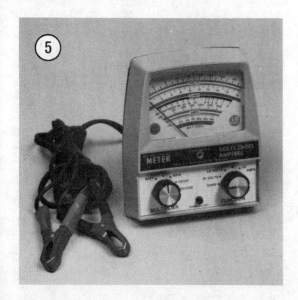

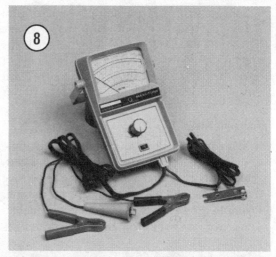

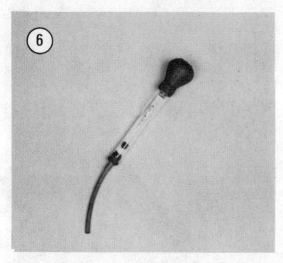

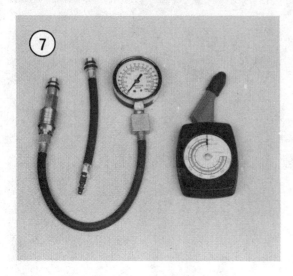

this angle is determined by breaker point gap, dwell angle is an accurate indication of breaker point gap.

Many tachometers intended for tuning and testing incorporate a dwell meter as well. See **Figure 8**. Follow the manufacturer's instructions to measure dwell.

Tachometer

A tachometer is necessary for tuning. See **Figure 8**. Ignition timing and carburetor adjustments must be performed at the specified idle speed. The best instrument for this purpose is one with a low range of 0-1,000 or 0-2,000 rpm for setting idle, and a high range of 0-4,000 or more for setting ignition timing at 3,000 rpm. Extended range (0-6,000 or 0-8,000 rpm) instruments lack accuracy at lower speeds. The instrument should be capable of detecting changes of 25 rpm on the low range.

NOTE: *The motorcycle's tachometer is not accurate enough for correct idle adjustment.*

Strobe Timing Light

This instrument is necessary for tuning, as it permits very accurate ignition timing. The light flashes at precisely the same instant that No. 1 cylinder fires, at which time the timing marks on the engine should align. Refer to Chapter Three for exact location of the timing marks for your engine.

Suitable lights range from inexpensive neon bulb types ($2-3) to powerful xenon strobe lights ($20-40). See **Figure 9**. Neon timing lights are difficult to see and must be used in dimly lit areas. Xenon strobe timing lights can be used outside in bright sunlight.

Tune-up Kits

Many manufacturers offer kits that combine several useful instruments. Some come in a convenient carry case and are usually less expensive than purchasing one instrument at a time. **Figure 10** shows one of the kits that is available. The prices vary with the number of instruments included in the kit.

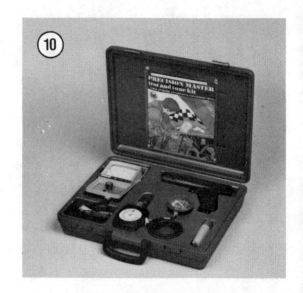

Manometer (Carburetor Synchronizer)

A manometer is essential for accurately synchronizing carburetors on multi-cylinder engines. The instrument detects intake pressure differences between carburetors and permits them to be adjusted equally. A suitable manometer costs about $25 and comes with detailed instructions for use. See **Figure 11**.

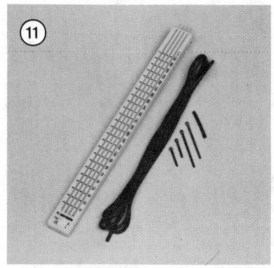

Fire Extinguisher

A fire extinguisher is a necessity when working on a vehicle. It should be rated for both *Class B* (flammable liquids — gasoline, oil, paint, etc.) and *Class C* (electrical — wiring, etc.) type fires. It should always be kept within reach. See **Figure 12**.

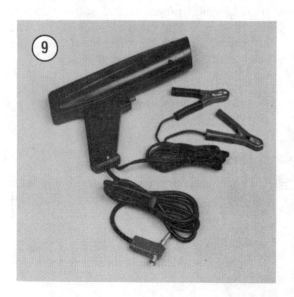

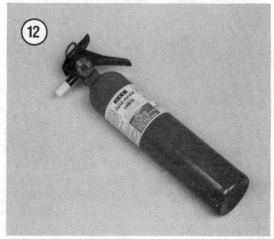

CHAPTER TWO

TROUBLESHOOTING

Troubleshooting motorcycle problems is relatively simple. To be effective and efficient, however, it must be done in a logical step-by-step manner. If it is not, a great deal of time may be wasted, good parts may be replaced unnecessarily, and the true problem may never be uncovered.

Always begin by defining the symptoms as closely as possible. Then, analyze the symptoms carefully so that you can make an intelligent guess at the probable cause. Next, test the probable cause and attempt to verify it; if it's not at fault, analyze the symptoms once again, this time eliminating the first probable cause. Continue on in this manner, a step at a time, until the problem is solved.

At first, this approach may seem to be time consuming, but you will soon discover that it's not nearly so wasteful as a hit-or-miss method that may never solve the problem. And just as important, the methodical approach to troubleshooting ensures that only those parts that are defective will be replaced.

The troubleshooting procedures in this chapter analyze typical symptoms and show logical methods for isolating and correcting trouble. They are not, however, the only methods; there may be several approaches to a given problem, but all good troubleshooting methods have one thing in common — a logical, systematic approach.

ENGINE

The entire engine must be considered when trouble arises that is experienced as poor performance or failure to start. The engine is more than a combustion chamber, piston, and crankshaft; it also includes a fuel delivery system, an ignition system, and an exhaust system.

Before beginning to troubleshoot any engine problems, it's important to understand an engine's operating requirements. First, it must have a correctly metered mixture of gasoline and air (**Figure 1**). Second, it must have an airtight combustion chamber in which the mixture can be compressed. And finally, it requires a precisely timed spark to ignite the compressed mixture. If one or more is missing, the engine won't run, and if just one is deficient, the engine will run poorly at best.

Of the three requirements, the precisely timed spark — provided by the ignition system — is most likely to be the culprit, with gas/air mixture (carburetion) second, and poor compression the least likely.

STARTING DIFFICULTIES

Hard starting is probably the most common motorcycle ailment, with a wide range of problems likely. Before delving into a reluctant or non-starter, first determine what has changed

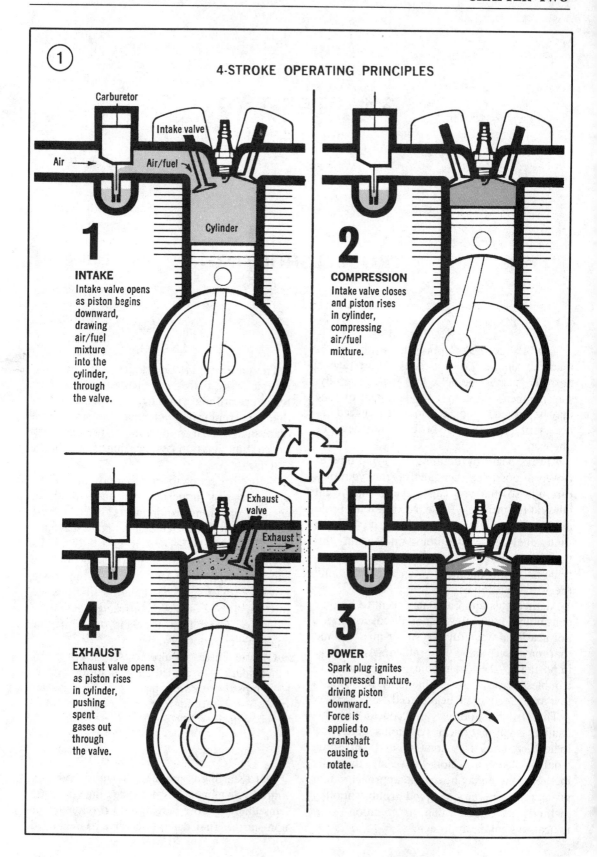

① 4-STROKE OPERATING PRINCIPLES

1 INTAKE
Intake valve opens as piston begins downward, drawing air/fuel mixture into the cylinder, through the valve.

2 COMPRESSION
Intake valve closes and piston rises in cylinder, compressing air/fuel mixture.

4 EXHAUST
Exhaust valve opens as piston rises in cylinder, pushing spent gases out through the valve.

3 POWER
Spark plug ignites compressed mixture, driving piston downward. Force is applied to crankshaft causing to rotate.

Labels: Carburetor, Intake valve, Air, Air/fuel, Cylinder, Exhaust valve, Exhaust

since the motorcycle last started easily. For in-stance, was the weather dry then and is it wet now? Has the motorcycle been sitting in the garage for a long time? Has it been ridden many miles since it was last fueled?

Has starting become increasingly more dif-ficult? This alone could indicate a number of things that may be wrong but is usually associated with normal wear of ignition and engine components.

While it's not always possible to diagnose trouble simply from a change of conditions, this information can be helpful and at some future time may uncover a recurring problem.

Fuel Delivery

Although it is the second most likely cause of trouble, fuel delivery should be checked first simply because it is the easiest.

First, check the tank to make sure there is fuel in it. Then, disconnect the fuel hose at the carburetor, open the valve and check for flow (**Figure 2**). If fuel does not flow freely make sure the tank vent is clear. Next, check for blockage in the line or valve. Remove the valve and clean it as described in the fuel system chapter.

If fuel flows from the hose, reconnect it and remove the float bowl from the carburetor, open the valve and check for flow through the float needle valve. If it does not flow freely when the float is extended and then shut off when the flow is gently raised, clean the car-buretor as described in the fuel system chapter.

When fuel delivery is satisfactory, go on to the ignition system.

Ignition

Remove the spark plug from the cylinder and check its condition. The appearance of the plug is a good indication of what's happening in the combustion chamber; for instance, if the plug is wet with gas, it's likely that engine is flooded. Compare the spark plug to **Figure 3**. Make cer-tain the spark plug heat range is correct. A "cold" plug makes starting difficult.

After checking the spark plug, reconnect it to the high-tension lead and lay it on the cylinder head so it makes good contact (**Figure 4**). Then, with the ignition switched on, crank the engine several times and watch for a spark across the plug electrodes. A fat, blue spark should be visible. If there is no spark, or if the spark is weak, substitute a good plug for the old one and check again. If the spark has improved, the old plug is faulty. If there was no change, keep looking.

Make sure the ignition switch is not shorted to ground. Remove the spark plug cap from the end of the high-tension lead and hold the ex-posed end of the lead about ⅛ inch from the cylinder head. Crank the engine and watch for a spark arcing from the lead to the head. If it's satisfactory, the connection between the lead and the cap was faulty. If the spark hasn't im-proved, check the coil wire connections.

If the spark is still weak, remove the ignition cover and remove any dirt or moisture from the points or sensor. Check the point or air gap against the specifications in the *Quick Reference Data* at the beginning of the book.

If spark is still not satisfactory, a more serious problem exists than can be corrected with simple adjustments. Refer to the electrical system chapter for detailed information for correcting major ignition problems.

Compression

Compression — or the lack of it — is the least likely cause of starting trouble. However, if compression is unsatisfactory, more than a simple adjustment is required to correct it (see the engine chapter).

An accurate compression check reveals a lot about the condition of the engine. To perform this test you need a compression gauge (see Chapter One). The engine should be at operating temperature for a fully accurate test, but even a cold test will reveal if the starting problem is compression.

Remove the spark plug and screw in a com-pression gauge (**Figure 5**). With assistance, hold the throttle wide open and crank the engine several times, until the gauge ceases to rise. Normal compression should be 130-160 psi, but a reading as low as 100 psi is usually sufficient for the engine to start. If the reading is much lower than normal, remove the gauge and pour about a tablespoon of oil into the cylinder.

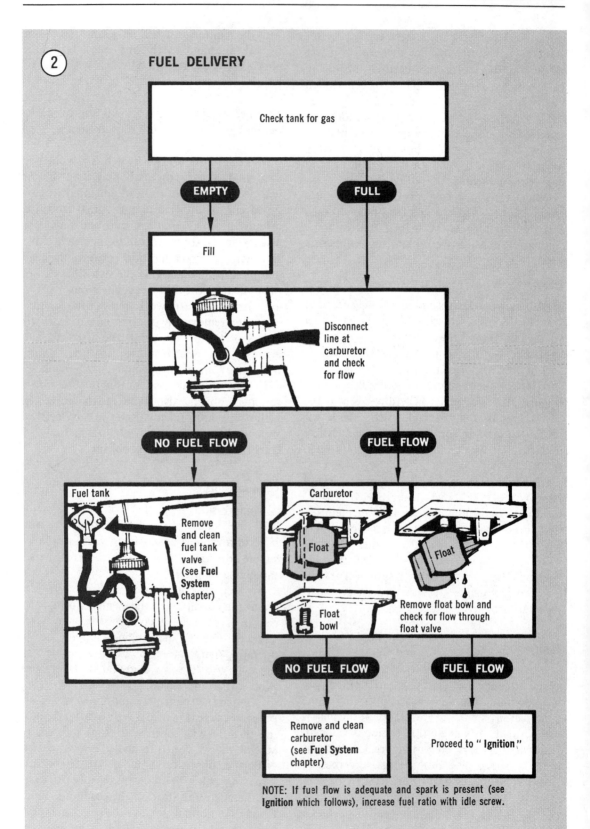

② FUEL DELIVERY

Check tank for gas

EMPTY

FULL

Fill

Disconnect line at carburetor and check for flow

NO FUEL FLOW

FUEL FLOW

Fuel tank

Remove and clean fuel tank valve (see **Fuel System** chapter)

Carburetor

Float

Float

Float bowl

Remove float bowl and check for flow through float valve

NO FUEL FLOW

FUEL FLOW

Remove and clean carburetor (see **Fuel System** chapter)

Proceed to " **Ignition**,"

NOTE: If fuel flow is adequate and spark is present (see **Ignition** which follows), increase fuel ratio with idle screw.

NORMAL
- Appearance—Firing tip has deposits of light gray to light tan.
- Can be cleaned, regapped and reused.

CARBON FOULED
- Appearance—Dull, dry black with fluffy carbon deposits on the insulator tip, electrode and exposed shell.
- Caused by—Fuel/air mixture too rich, plug heat range too cold, weak ignition system, dirty air cleaner, faulty automatic choke or excessive idling.
- Can be cleaned, regapped and reused.

OIL FOULED
- Appearance—Wet black deposits on insulator and exposed shell.
- Caused by—Excessive oil entering the combustion chamber through worn rings, pistons, valve guides or bearings.
- Replace with new plugs (use a hotter plug if engine is not repaired).

LEAD FOULED
- Appearance — Yellow insulator deposits (may sometimes be dark gray, black or tan in color) on the insulator tip.
- Caused by—Highly leaded gasoline.
- Replace with new plugs.

LEAD FOULED
- Appearance—Yellow glazed deposits indicating melted lead deposits due to hard acceleration.
- Caused by—Highly leaded gasoline.
- Replace with new plugs.

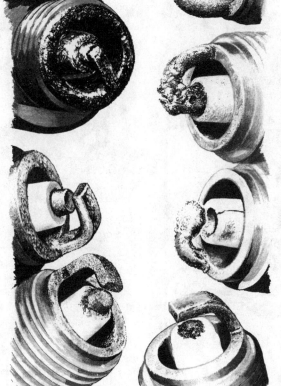

OIL AND LEAD FOULED
- Appearance—Glazed yellow deposits with a slight brownish tint on the insulator tip and ground electrode.
- Replace with new plugs.

FUEL ADDITIVE RESIDUE
- Appearance — Brown colored hardened ash deposits on the insulator tip and ground electrode.
- Caused by—Fuel and/or oil additives.
- Replace with new plugs.

WORN
- Appearance — Severely worn or eroded electrodes.
- Caused by—Normal wear or unusual oil and/or fuel additives.
- Replace with new plugs.

PREIGNITION
- Appearance — Melted ground electrode.
- Caused by—Overadvanced ignition timing, inoperative ignition advance mechanism, too low of a fuel octane rating, lean fuel/air mixture or carbon deposits in combustion chamber.

PREIGNITION
- Appearance—Melted center electrode.
- Caused by—Abnormal combustion due to overadvanced ignition timing or incorrect advance, too low of a fuel octane rating, lean fuel/air mixture, or carbon deposits in combustion chamber.
- Correct engine problem and replace with new plugs.

INCORRECT HEAT RANGE
- Appearance—Melted center electrode and white blistered insulator tip.
- Caused by—Incorrect plug heat range selection.
- Replace with new plugs.

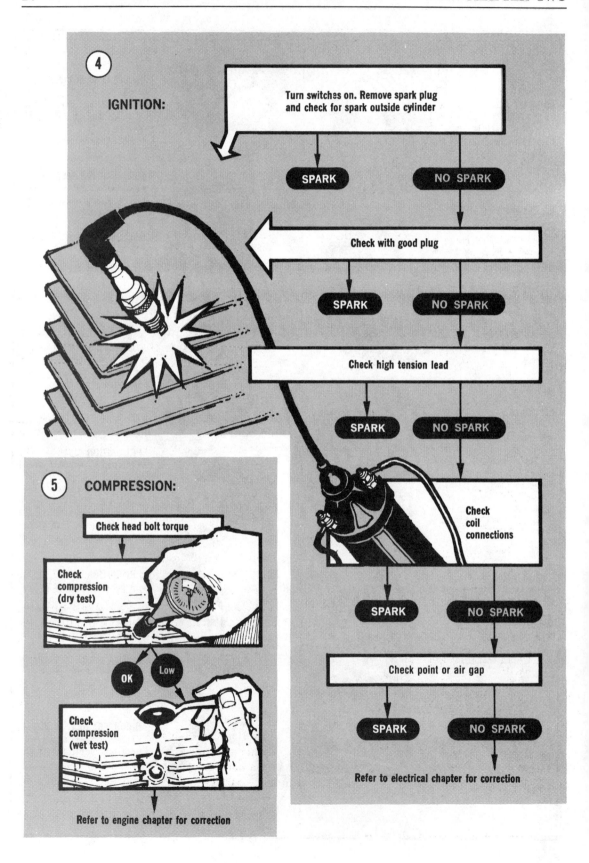

(4)

IGNITION:

Turn switches on. Remove spark plug and check for spark outside cylinder

SPARK   NO SPARK

Check with good plug

SPARK   NO SPARK

Check high tension lead

SPARK   NO SPARK

Check coil connections

SPARK   NO SPARK

Check point or air gap

SPARK   NO SPARK

Refer to electrical chapter for correction

(5) COMPRESSION:

Check head bolt torque

Check compression (dry test)

OK   Low

Check compression (wet test)

Refer to engine chapter for correction

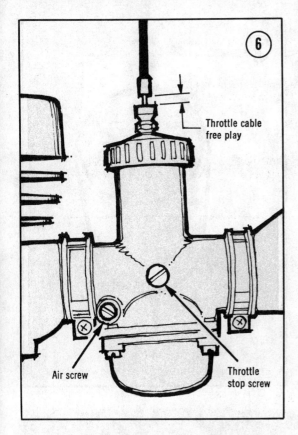

Throttle cable
free play

Air screw

Throttle
stop screw

Crank the engine several times to distribute the oil and test the compression once again. If it is now significantly higher, the rings and bore are worn. If the compression did not change, the valves are not seating correctly. Adjust the valves and check again. If the compression is still low, refer to the engine chapter.

> NOTE: *Low compression indicates a developing problem. The condition causing it should be corrected as soon as possible.*

POOR PERFORMANCE

Poor engine performance can be caused by any of a number of things related to carburetion, ignition, and the condition of the sliding and rotating components in the engine. In addition, components such as brakes, clutch, and transmission can cause problems that seem to be related to engine performance, even when the engine is in top running condition.

Poor Idling

Idling that is erratic, too high, or too low is most often caused by incorrect adjustment of the carburetor idle circuit. Also, a dirty air filter or an obstructed fuel tank vent can affect idle speed. Incorrect ignition timing or worn or faulty ignition components are also good possibilities.

First, make sure the air filter is clean and correctly installed. Then, adjust the throttle cable free play, the throttle stop screw, and the idle mixture air screw (**Figure 6**) as described in the routine maintenance chapter.

If idling is still poor, check the carburetor and manifold mounts for leaks; with the engine warmed up and running, spray WD-40 or a similar light lube around the flanges and joints of the carburetor and manifold (**Figure 7**). Listen for changes in engine speed. If a leak is present, the idle speed will drop as the lube "plugs" the leak and then pick up again as it is drawn into the engine. Tighten the nuts and clamps and test again. If a leak persists, check for a damaged gasket or a pinhole in the manifold. Minor leaks in manifold hoses can be repaired with silicone sealer, but if cracks or holes are extensive, the manifold should be replaced.

A worn throttle slide may cause erratic running and idling, but this is likely only after many thousands of miles of use. To check, remove the carburetor top and feel for back and forth movement of the slide in the bore; it should be barely perceptible. Inspect the slide for large worn areas and replace it if it is less than perfect (**Figure 8**).

If the fuel system is satisfactory, check ignition timing and breaker point gap (air gap in electronic ignition). Check the condition of the system components as well. Ignition-caused idling problems such as erratic running can be the fault of marginal components. See the electrical system chapter for appropriate tests.

Rough Running or Misfiring

Misfiring (see **Figure 9**) is usually caused by an ignition problem. First, check all ignition connections (**Figure 10**). They should be clean, dry, and tight. Don't forget the kill switch; a loose connection can create an intermittent short.

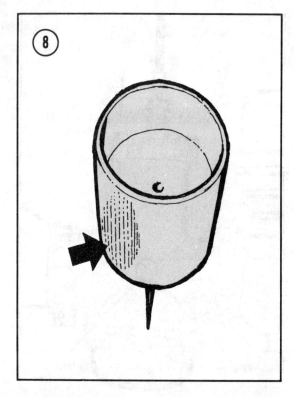

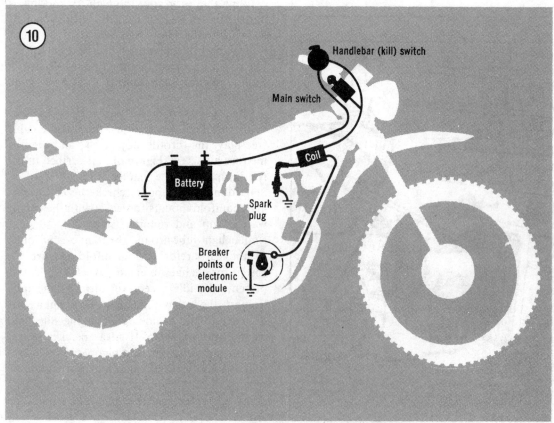

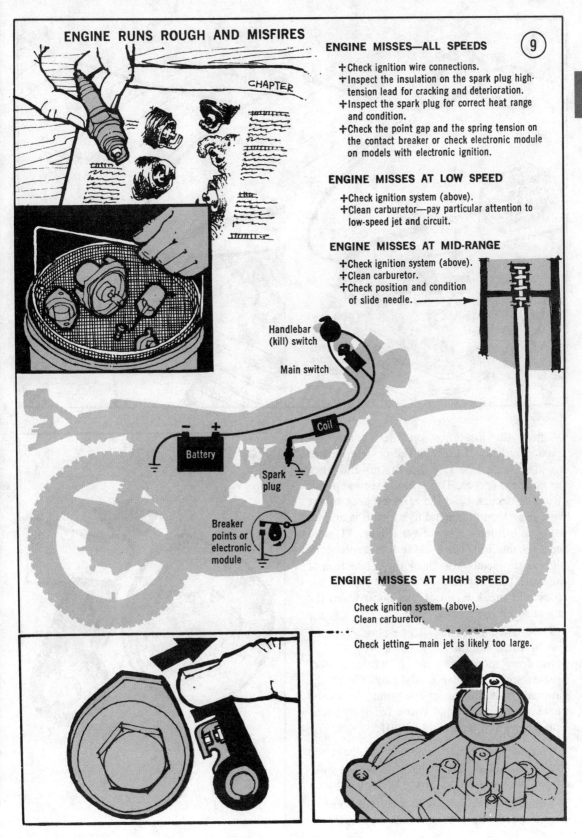

ENGINE RUNS ROUGH AND MISFIRES

CHAPTER

ENGINE MISSES—ALL SPEEDS ⑨

+ Check ignition wire connections.
+ Inspect the insulation on the spark plug high-tension lead for cracking and deterioration.
+ Inspect the spark plug for correct heat range and condition.
+ Check the point gap and the spring tension on the contact breaker or check electronic module on models with electronic ignition.

ENGINE MISSES AT LOW SPEED

+ Check ignition system (above).
+ Clean carburetor—pay particular attention to low-speed jet and circuit.

ENGINE MISSES AT MID-RANGE

+ Check ignition system (above).
+ Clean carburetor.
+ Check position and condition of slide needle. →

Handlebar (kill) switch

Main switch

Coil

Battery

Spark plug

Breaker points or electronic module

ENGINE MISSES AT HIGH SPEED

Check ignition system (above).
Clean carburetor.

Check jetting—main jet is likely too large.

2

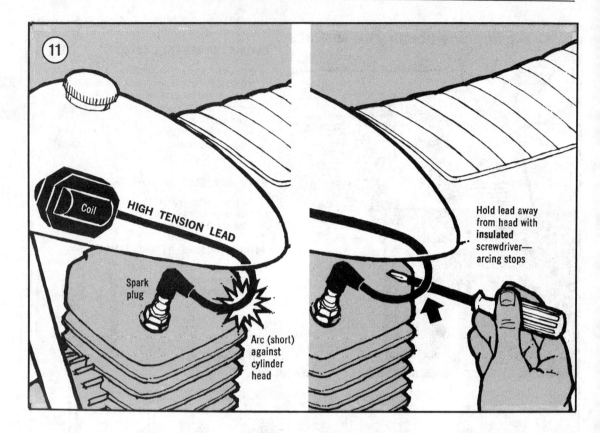

Check the insulation on the high-tension spark plug lead. If it is cracked or deteriorated it will allow the spark to short to ground when the engine is revved. This is easily seen at night. If arcing occurs, hold the affected area of the wire away from the metal to which it is arcing, using an insulated screwdriver (**Figure 11**), and see if the misfiring ceases. If it does, replace the high-tension lead. Also check the connection of the spark plug cap to the lead. If it is poor, the spark will break down at this point when the engine speed is increased.

The spark plug could also be poor. Test the system with a new plug.

Incorrect point gap or a weak contact breaker spring can cause misfiring. Check the gap and the alignment of the points. Push the moveable arm back and check for spring tension (**Figure 12**). It should feel stiff.

On models with electronic ignition, have the electronic module tested by a dealer or substitute a known good unit for a suspected one.

If misfiring occurs only at a certain point in engine speed, the problem may very likely be

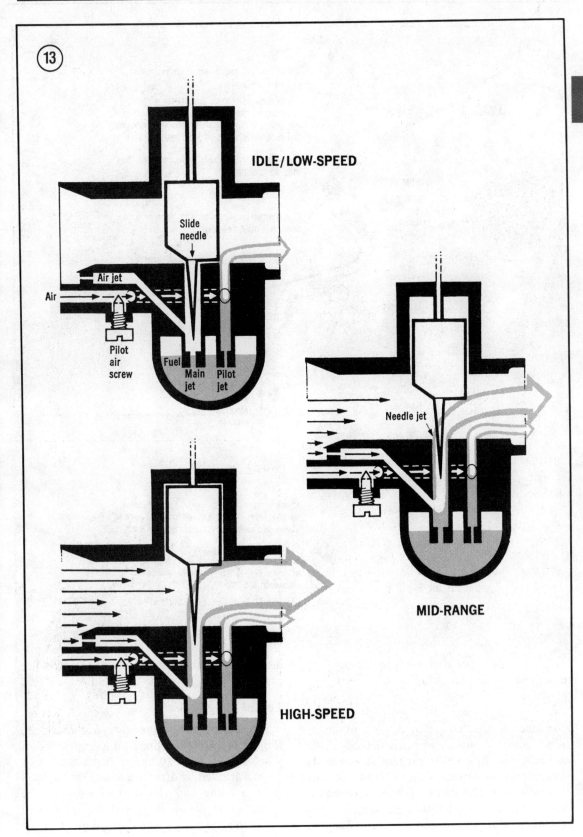

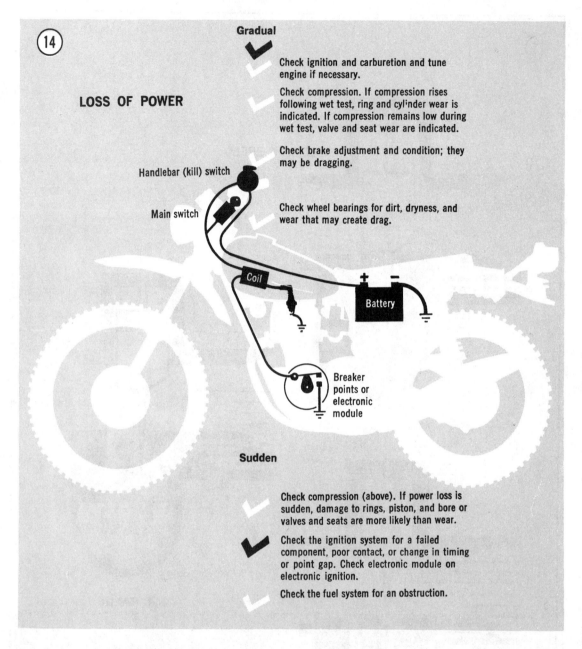

⑭

Gradual

LOSS OF POWER

Check ignition and carburetion and tune engine if necessary.

Check compression. If compression rises following wet test, ring and cylinder wear is indicated. If compression remains low during wet test, valve and seat wear are indicated.

Check brake adjustment and condition; they may be dragging.

Handlebar (kill) switch

Main switch

Check wheel bearings for dirt, dryness, and wear that may create drag.

Coil

Battery

Breaker points or electronic module

Sudden

Check compression (above). If power loss is sudden, damage to rings, piston, and bore or valves and seats are more likely than wear.

Check the ignition system for a failed component, poor contact, or change in timing or point gap. Check electronic module on electronic ignition.

Check the fuel system for an obstruction.

carburetion. Poor performance at idle is described earlier. Misfiring at low speed (just above idle) can be caused by a dirty low-speed circuit or jet (**Figure 13**). Poor midrange performance is attributable to a worn or incorrectly adjusted needle and needle jet. Misfiring at high speed (if not ignition related) is usually caused by a too-large main jet which causes the engine to run rich. Any of these carburetor-related conditions can be corrected by first cleaning the carburetor and then adjusting it as described in the tune-up and maintenance chapter.

Loss of Power

First determine how the power loss developed (**Figure 14**). Did it decline over a long period of time or did it drop abruptly? A gradual loss is normal, caused by deterioration of the engine's state of tune and the normal wear of the cylinder and piston rings and the valves and seats. In such case, check the condition of the

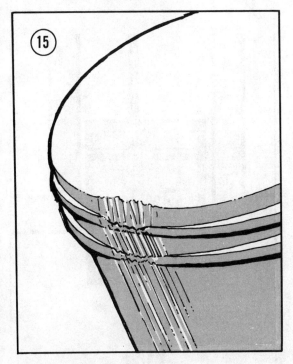

ignition and carburetion and measure the compression as described earlier.

A sudden power loss may be caused by a failed ignition component, obstruction in the fuel system, damaged valve or seat, or a broken piston ring or damaged piston (**Figure 15**).

If the engine is in good shape and tune, check the brake adjustment. If the brakes are dragging, they will consume considerable power. Also check the wheel bearings. If they are dry, extremely dirty, or badly worn they can create considerable drag.

Engine Runs Hot

A modern motorcycle engine, in good mechanical condition, correctly tuned, and operated as it was intended, will rarely experience overheating problems. However, out-of-spec conditions can create severe overheating that may result in serious engine damage. Refer to **Figure 16**.

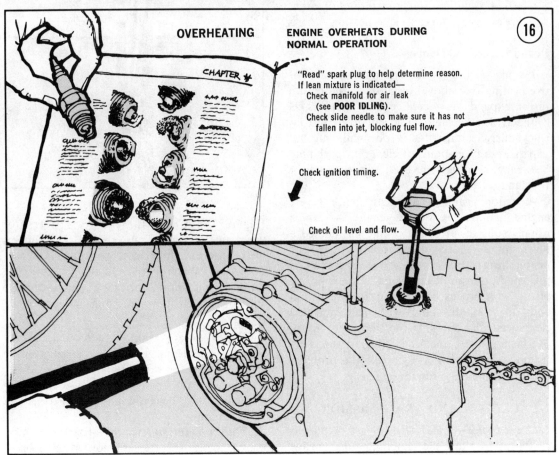

OVERHEATING

ENGINE OVERHEATS DURING NORMAL OPERATION

"Read" spark plug to help determine reason.
If lean mixture is indicated—
  Check manifold for air leak
    (see **POOR IDLING**).
  Check slide needle to make sure it has not fallen into jet, blocking fuel flow.

Check ignition timing.

Check oil level and flow.

Overheating is difficult to detect unless it is extreme, in which case it will usually be apparent as excessive heat radiating from the engine, accompanied by the smell of hot oil and sharp, snapping noises when the engine is first shut off and begins to cool.

Unless the motorcycle is operated under sustained high load or is allowed to idle for long periods of time, overheating is usually the result of an internal problem. Most often it's caused by a too-lean fuel mixture.

Remove the spark plug and compare it to **Figure 3**. If a too-lean condition is indicated, check for leaks in the intake manifold (see *Poor Idling*). The carburetor jetting may be incorrect but this is unlikely if the overheating problem has just developed (unless, of course, the engine was jetted for high altitude and is now being run near sea level). Check the slide needle in the carburetor to make sure it hasn't come loose and is restricting the flow of gas through the main jet and needle jet (**Figure 17**).

Check the ignition timing; extremes of either advance or retard can cause overheating.

Piston Seizure and Damage

Piston seizure is a common result of overheating (see above) because an aluminum piston expands at a greater rate than a steel cylinder. Seizure can also be caused by piston-to-cylinder clearance that is too small; ring end gap that is too small; insufficient oil; spark plug heat range too hot; and broken piston ring or ring land.

A major piston seizure can cause severe engine damage. A minor seizure — which usually subsides after the engine has cooled a few minutes — rarely does more than scuff the piston skirt the first time it occurs. Fortunately, this condition can be corrected by dressing the piston with crocus cloth, refitting the piston and rings to the bore with recommended clearances, and checking the timing to ensure overheating does not occur. Regard that first seizure as a warning and correct the problem before continuing to run the engine.

CLUTCH AND TRANSMISSION

1. *Clutch slips*—Make sure lever free play is sufficient to allow the clutch to fully engage

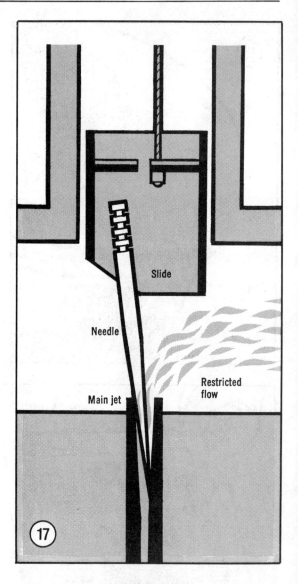

Slide

Needle

Main jet

Restricted flow

(17)

(**Figure 18**). Check the contact surfaces for wear and glazing. Transmission oil additives also can cause slippage in wet clutches. If slip occurs only under extreme load, check the condition of the springs or diaphragm and make sure the clutch bolts are snug and uniformly tightened.

2. *Clutch drags*—Make sure lever free play isn't so great that it fails to disengage the clutch. Check for warped plates or disc. If the transmission oil (in wet clutch systems) is extremely dirty or heavy, it may inhibit the clutch from releasing.

3. *Transmission shifts hard*—Extremely dirty oil can cause the transmission to shift hard.

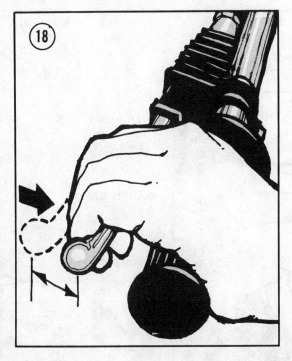

Check the selector shaft for bending (**Figure 19**). Inspect the shifter and gearsets for wear and damage.

4. *Transmission slips out of gear*—This can be caused by worn engagement dogs or a worn or damaged shifter (**Figure 20**). The overshift travel on the selector may be misadjusted.

5. *Transmission is noisy*—Noises usually indicate the absence of lubrication or wear and damage to gears, bearings, or shims. It's a good idea to disassemble the transmission and carefully inspect it when noise first occurs.

DRIVE TRAIN

Drive train problems (outlined in **Figure 21**) arise from normal wear and incorrect maintenance.

CHASSIS

Chassis problems are outlined in **Figure 22**.

1. *Motorcycle pulls to one side*—Check for loose suspension components, axles, steering

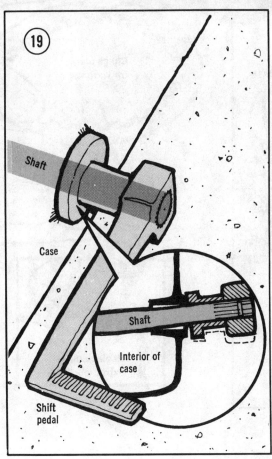

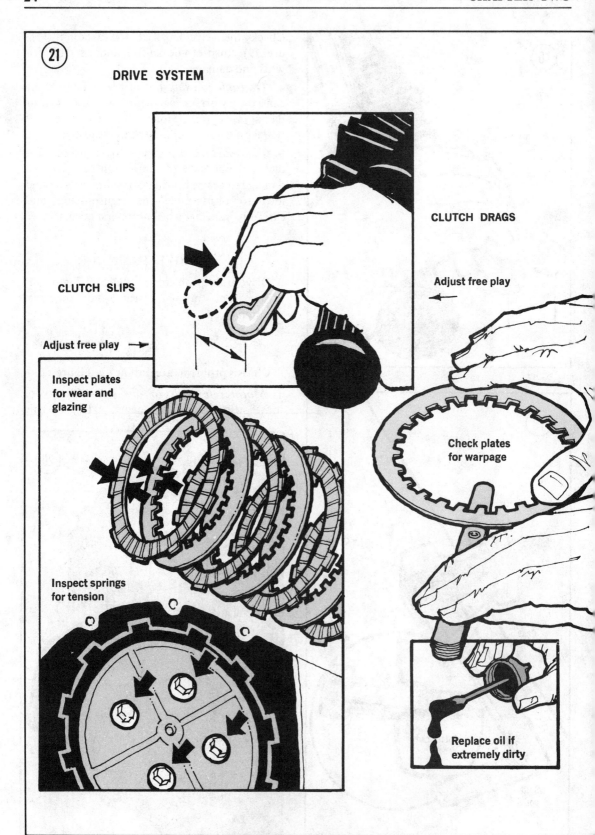

(21)

DRIVE SYSTEM

CLUTCH DRAGS

CLUTCH SLIPS

Adjust free play

Adjust free play

Inspect plates
for wear and
glazing

Check plates
for warpage

Inspect springs
for tension

Replace oil if
extremely dirty

2

TRANSMISSION SLIPS OUT OF GEAR

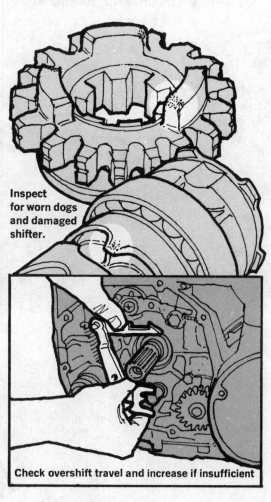

Inspect
for worn dogs
and damaged
shifter.

TRANSMISSION SHIFTS HARD

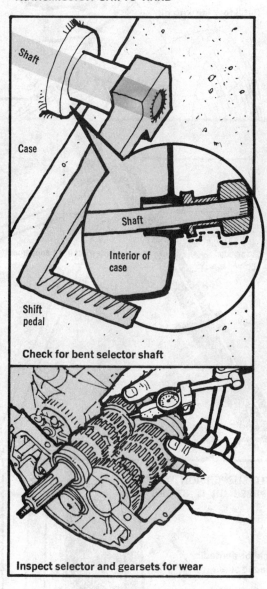

Shaft

Case

Shaft

Interior of
case

Shift
pedal

Check for bent selector shaft

Inspect selector and gearsets for wear

Check overshift travel and increase if insufficient

TRANSMISSION IS NOISY

Check oil level

Disassemble and inspect (see Transmission
chapter)

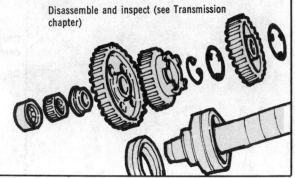

㉒

SUSPENSION AND HANDLING

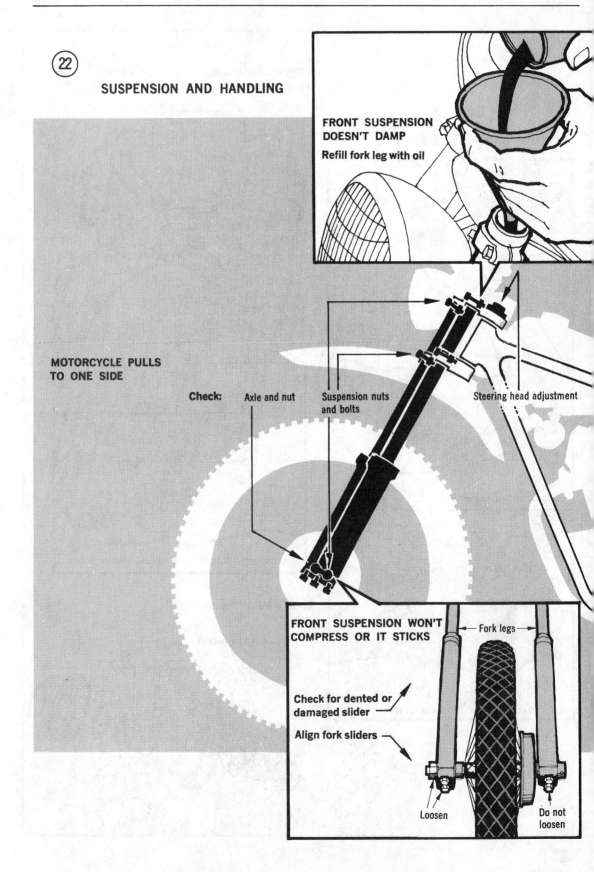

FRONT SUSPENSION
DOESN'T DAMP
Refill fork leg with oil

**MOTORCYCLE PULLS
TO ONE SIDE**

Check: Axle and nut   Suspension nuts   Steering head adjustment
                                and bolts

FRONT SUSPENSION WON'T
COMPRESS OR IT STICKS   ← Fork legs →

**Check for dented or
damaged slider**

Align fork sliders

Loosen   Do not
                                                loosen

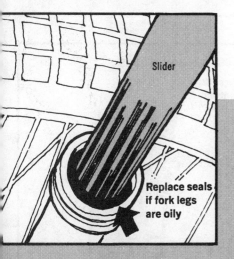

Slider

Replace seals
if fork legs
are oily

SUSPENSION AND HANDLING CONTINUED ⟹ 2

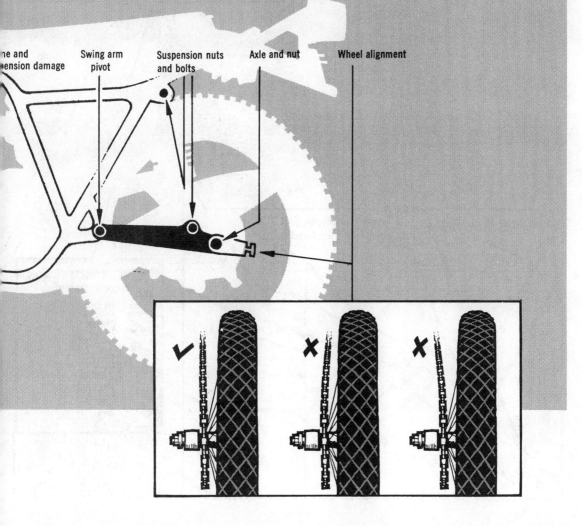

...me and   Swing arm   Suspension nuts   Axle and nut   Wheel alignment
...ension damage   pivot   and bolts

SUSPENSION AND HANDLING CONTINUED

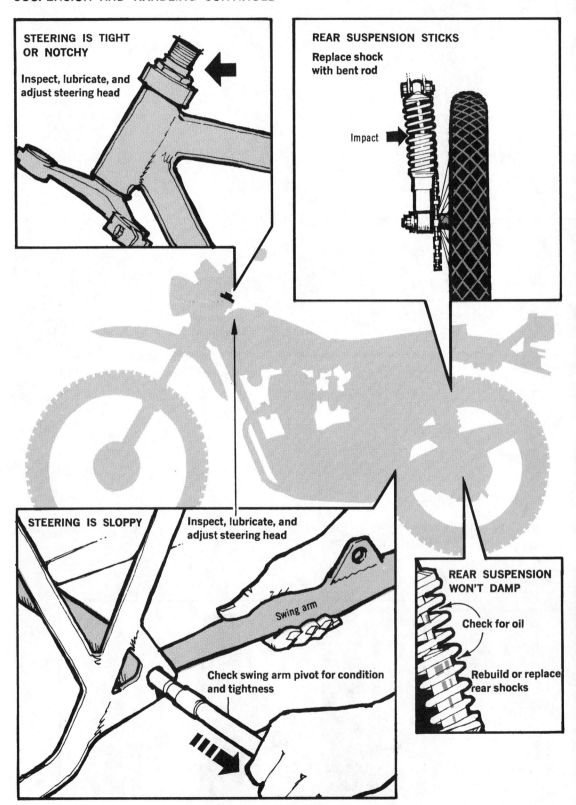

STEERING IS TIGHT OR NOTCHY

Inspect, lubricate, and adjust steering head

REAR SUSPENSION STICKS

Replace shock with bent rod

Impact

Inspect, lubricate, and adjust steering head

STEERING IS SLOPPY

Swing arm

Check swing arm pivot for condition and tightness

REAR SUSPENSION WON'T DAMP

Check for oil

Rebuild or replace rear shocks

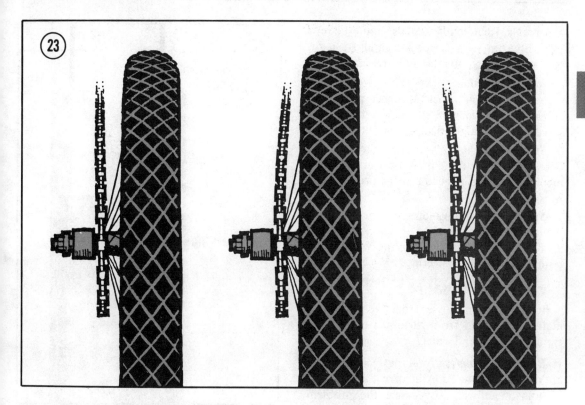

head, swing arm pivot. Check wheel alignment (**Figure 23**). Check for damage to the frame and suspension components.

2. *Front suspension doesn't damp*—This is most often caused by a lack of damping oil in the fork legs. If the upper fork tubes are exceptionally oily, it's likely that the seals are worn out and should be replaced.

3. *Front suspension sticks or won't fully compress*—Misalignment of the forks when the wheel is installed can cause this. Loosen the axle nut and the pinch bolt on the nut end of the axle (**Figure 24**). Lock the front wheel with the brake and compress the front suspension several times to align the fork legs. Then, tighten the pinch bolt and then the axle nut.

The trouble may also be caused by a bent or dented fork slider (**Figure 25**). The distortion required to lock up a fork tube is so slight that it is often impossible to visually detect. If this type of damage is suspected, remove the fork leg and remove the spring from it. Attempt to operate the fork leg. If it still binds, replace the slider; it's not practical to repair it.

4. *Rear suspension does not damp*—This is usually caused by damping oil leaking past

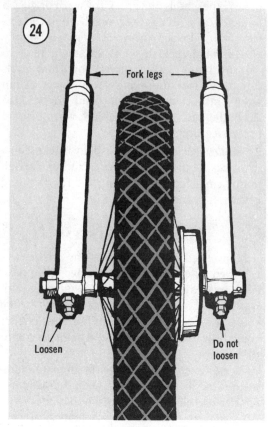

Fork legs

Loosen

Do not loosen

worn seals. Rebuildable shocks should be refitted with complete service kits and fresh oil. Non-rebuildable units should be replaced.

5. *Rear suspension sticks*—This is commonly caused by a bent shock absorber piston rod (**Figure 26**). Replace the shock; the rod can't be satisfactorily straightened.

6. *Steering is tight or "notchy"*—Steering head bearings may be dry, dirty, or worn. Adjustment of the steering head bearing pre-load may be too tight.

7. *Steering is sloppy*—Steering head adjustment may be too loose. Also check the swing arm pivot; looseness or extreme wear at this point translate to the steering.

BRAKES

Brake problems arise from wear, lack of maintenance, and from sustained or repeated exposure to dirt and water.

1. *Brakes are ineffective*—Ineffective brakes are most likely caused by incorrect adjustment. If adjustment will not correct the problem, remove the wheels and check for worn or glazed linings. If the linings are worn beyond the service limit, replace them. If they are simply glazed, rough them up with light sandpaper.

In hydraulic brake systems, low fluid levels can cause a loss of braking effectiveness, as can worn brake cylinder pistons and bores. Also check the pads to see if they are worn beyond the service limit.

2. *Brakes lock or drag*—This may be caused by incorrect adjustment. Check also for foreign matter embedded in the lining and for dirty and dry wheel bearings.

ELECTRICAL SYSTEM

Many electrical system problems can be easily solved by ensuring that the affected connections are clean, dry, and tight. In battery equipped motorcycles, a neglected battery is the source of a great number of difficulties that could be prevented by simple, regular service to the battery.

A multimeter, like the volt/ohm/milliammeter described in Chapter One, is invaluable for efficient electrical system troubleshooting.

See **Figures 27 and 28** for schematics showing

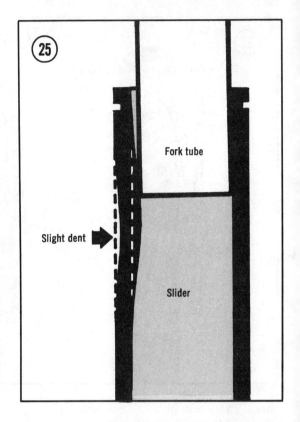

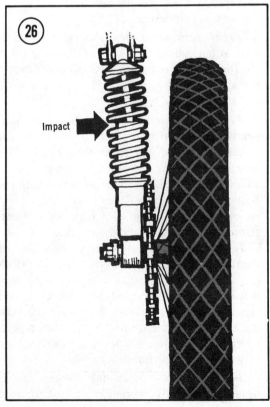

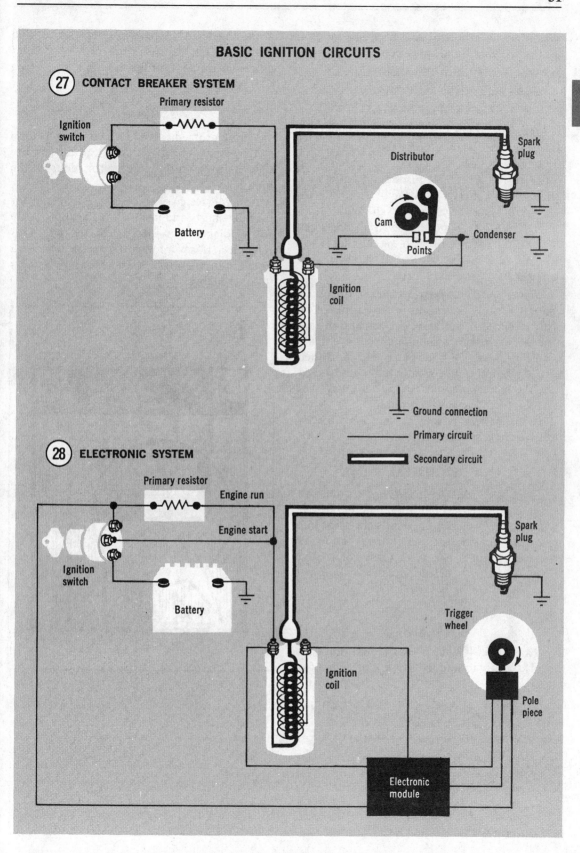

BASIC IGNITION CIRCUITS

27 CONTACT BREAKER SYSTEM

Primary resistor

Ignition switch

Battery

Distributor

Cam

Points

Condenser

Spark plug

Ignition coil

⏚ Ground connection

—— Primary circuit

▭ Secondary circuit

28 ELECTRONIC SYSTEM

Primary resistor

Engine run

Engine start

Ignition switch

Battery

Ignition coil

Spark plug

Trigger wheel

Pole piece

Electronic module

simplified conventional and electronic ignition systems. Typical and most common electrical troubles are also described.

CHARGING SYSTEM

1. *Battery will not accept a charge*—Make sure the electrolyte level in the battery is correct and that the terminal connections are tight and free of corrosion. Check for fuses in the battery circuit. If the battery is satisfactory, refer to the electrical system chapter for alternator tests. Finally, keep in mind that even a good alternator is not capable of restoring the charge to a severely discharged battery; it must first be charged by an external source.

2. *Battery will not hold a charge*—Check the battery for sulfate deposits in the bottom of the case (**Figure 29**). Sulfation occurs naturally and the deposits will accumulate and eventually come in contact with the plates and short them out. Sulfation can be greatly retarded by keeping the battery well charged at all times. Test the battery to assess its condition.

If the battery is satisfactory, look for excessive draw, such as a short.

LIGHTING

Bulbs burn out frequently—All bulbs will eventually burn out, but if the bulb in one particular light burns out frequently check the light assembly for looseness that may permit excessive vibration; check for loose connections that could cause current surges; check also to make sure the bulb is of the correct rating.

FUSES

Fuse blows—When a fuse blows, don't just replace it; try to find the cause. Consider a fuse

a warning device as well as a safety device. And never replace a fuse with one of greater amperage rating. It probably won't melt before the insulation on the wiring does.

WIRING

Wiring problems should be corrected as soon as they arise — before a short can cause a fire that may seriously damage or destroy the motorcycle.

A circuit tester of some type is essential for locating shorts and opens. Use the appropriate wiring diagram at the end of the book for reference. If a wire must be replaced make a notation on the wiring diagram of any changes in color coding.

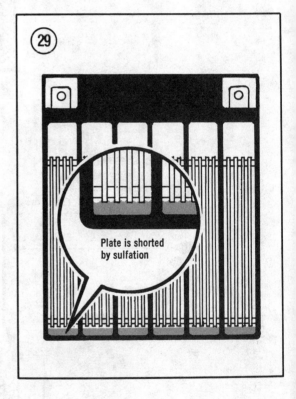

Plate is shorted by sulfation

CHAPTER THREE

LUBRICATION AND MAINTENANCE

To gain the utmost in safety, performance and useful life from your motorcycle, it is necessary to make periodic inspections and adjustments. It frequently happens that minor problems found during such inspections are simple and inexpensive to correct at the time, but could lead to major failures later. This chapter describes such services.

Table 1 is a suggested maintenance schedule.

ENGINE TUNE-UP

The purpose of a tune-up is to restore power and performance lost over a gradual period of time due to normal wear.

Carry out the tune-up in the same sequence as in this chapter for best results.

Cam Chain Tensioner

Engine valves and breaker points are opened and closed by a chain-driven camshaft. Wear in this chain results in altered valve and ignition timing, so it is necessary to adjust chain tension periodically.

1. Remove the alternator cover (**Figure 1**).
2. Remove the tappet covers (**Figure 2**).

3. Using a wrench on the alternator rotor bolt, turn the engine counterclockwise until the left cylinder intake valve opens fully, then starts to close. Continue turning engine from this point until the LT mark on the alternator rotor aligns with its index pointer (**Figure 3**).

NOTE
The piston in the left cylinder is at top dead center (TDC) on the compression stroke. A cylinder at TDC will have both its rocker

arms loose, indicating that both the intake and exhaust valves are closed. If both rockers are not loose, rotate the crankshaft counterclockwise 360° and realign the LT mark.

4. Loosen the locknut and the tensioner bolt (**Figure 4**). Chain slack will automatically be taken up by the tensioner mechanism.

5. Tighten the tensioner bolt and locknut. This locks the internal plunger in position.

Valve Clearance

The rocker arms have non-adjustable tappets. To adjust the valves proceed as follows.

1. Remove all tappet covers (A, **Figure 5**) and the contact breaker point cover (B, **Figure 5**).

2. Remove the alternator cover (**Figure 1**).

3. Using a wrench on the alternator rotor bolt, turn the engine counterclockwise until the left cylinder intake valve opens fully, then starts to close. Continue turning engine from this point until the LT mark on the alternator rotor aligns with its index pointer (**Figure 3**).

> *NOTE*
> *The piston in the left cylinder is at top dead center (TDC) on the compression stroke.*

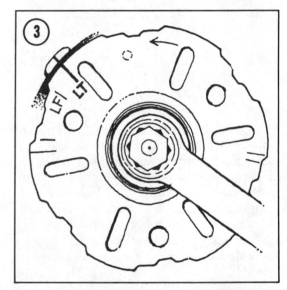

Table 1   MAINTENANCE SCHEDULE

Maintenance Item	Miles		
	1,000	3,000	6,000
Engine tune-up		X	
Check battery	X		
Change oil	X	X	X
Service oil filter			X
Adjust clutch		X	
Check lights and horn	X		
Adjust chain	X		
Adjust brakes	X		
Check brake lining			X
Check wheels	X		
Check tires	X		
Change fork oil		X	
Grease wheel bearings			X
Check steering bearings			X
Grease swing arm		X	

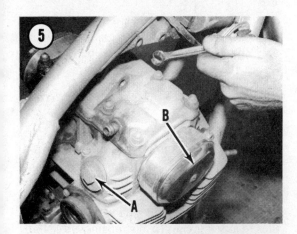

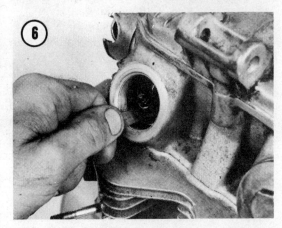

A cylinder at TDC will have both its rocker arms loose, indicating that both the intake and exhaust valves are closed. If both rockers are not loose, rotate the crankshaft counterclockwise 360° and realign the LT mark.

4. On the left cylinder, measure clearance between cam follower and the valve stem, using a flat feeler gauge (**Figure 6**). Intake valve clearance should be 0.002 in. (0.05mm) and exhaust valve clearance should be 0.004 in. (0.10mm).

5. If clearance is incorrect, refer to **Figure 7**. Loosen locknut (A), then turn adjuster (B) as required until clearance is as specified. Hold the adjuster in position and tighten the locknut.

6. Recheck the clearance and readjust if necessary.

7. Turn the alternator rotor bolt counter-clockwise 180° until the T mark on the alternator rotor aligns with its index mark (**Figure 8**).

8. Repeat Steps 4-6 and measure and adjust (if necessary) the valves on the right cylinder.

3

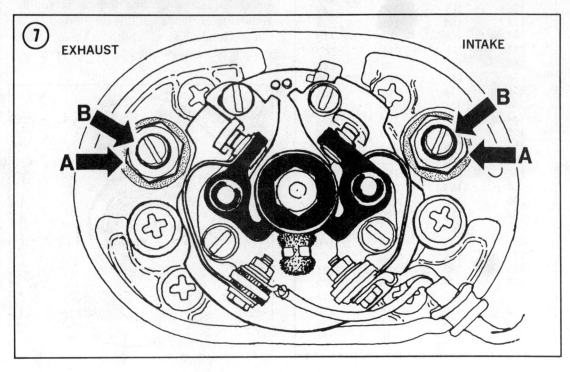

Compression Test

An engine requires adequate compression to develop full power. If for any reason compression is low, the engine will not develop full power. A compression test or, even better, a series of them over the life of the motorcycle, will tell much about engine condition.

To carry out a compression test, proceed as follows:

1. Start the engine, then ride the bike long enough to warm it thoroughly.
2. Remove each spark plug (refer to *Spark Plug Inspection and Service*, following section).
3. Screw a compression gauge into the spark plug hole, or if a press-in type gauge is used, hold it firmly in position (**Figure 9**).
4. With the ignition switch OFF, and the throttle wide open, crank the engine briskly with the kickstarter several times; the

compression gauge indication will increase with each kick. Continue to crank the engine until the gauge shows no more increase, then record the gauge indication. For example, on the first kick the gauge might indicate 90 psi; the second kick, 140 psi; the third kick, 160 psi, etc.

5. Repeat this procedure for the remaining cylinder. Normal compression at sea level will be about 140-170 psi, decreasing with altitude.

A sudden drop in cylinder compression could be caused by many factors, most of which require major engine service. Some of these causes are worn piston rings, a leaking cylinder head gasket, or a leaking valve.

A quick check for worn piston rings is easy: pour a spoonful of heavy engine oil through the spark plug opening. The oil will flow over the head of the piston, temporarily sealing the piston rings. Repeat the compression test for that cylinder. If the compression comes up to normal (or near normal), it is an indication that the rings are worn, or the cylinder is defective.

If the compression remains low after pouring oil into the spark plug hole and repeating the compression test, it is likely that a valve or head gasket is leaking. (A rapid on-off squeal when the engine is running frequently accompanies this condition.)

On Honda Twins, a difference of 25% in compression measurements between cylinders

Table 2   COMPRESSION PRESSURE LIMITS

Pressure (psi)		Pressure (psi)	
Maximum	Minimum	Maximum	Minimum
134	101	188	141
136	102	190	142
138	104	192	144
140	105	194	145
142	107	196	147
146	110	198	148
148	111	200	150
150	113	202	151
152	114	204	153
154	115	206	154
156	117	208	156
158	118	210	157
160	120	212	158
162	121	214	160
164	123	216	162
166	124	218	163
168	126	220	165
170	127	222	166
172	129	224	168
174	131	226	169
176	132	228	171
178	133	230	172
180	135	232	174
182	136	234	175
184	138	236	177
186	140	238	178

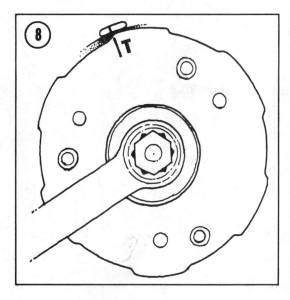

should be taken as an indication that engine repairs should be made. Likewise, a difference of 25% between successive measurements on any cylinder over a period of time (if made under identical conditions) is also an indication of trouble.

Table 2 may be used as a quick reference when checking cylinder compression pressures. It has been calculated so that the lowest reading number is 75% of the highest reading number.

Example: After checking the compression pressures in all cylinders it was found that the highest pressure obtained was 150 psi. The lowest pressure reading was 140 psi. By locating 150 in the maximum column, it is seen that the minimum allowable pressure is 113 psi. Since the lowest reading obtained was 140 psi, the compression is within satisfactory limits.

Spark Plug Inspection and Service

Spark plugs are available in various heat ranges hotter or colder than the spark plug originally installed at the factory.

Select plugs of a heat range designed for the loads and temperature conditions under which the engine will run. Use of incorrect heat ranges can cause seized pistons, scored cylinder walls, or damaged piston crowns.

In general, use a low-numbered plug for low speeds, low loads, and low temperatures. Use a higher-numbered plug for high speeds, high engine loads, and high temperatures.

> NOTE: *Use the highest numbered plug that will not foul. In areas where seasonal temperature variations are great, the factory recommends a high-numbered plug for slower winter operation.*

The reach (length) of a plug is also important. A longer-than-normal plug could interfere with the piston, causing severe damage. Refer to **Figures 10** and **Figure 11**.

Spark plugs of the correct heat range, with the engine in a proper state of tune, will appear light tan. See **Figure 12** for the various spark plug conditions you might encounter.

Changing spark plugs is generally a simple operation. Occasionally heat and corrosion can cause the plug to bind in the cylinder head, making removal difficult. Do not use force; the head is easily damaged. Here is the proper way to replace a plug.

1. Blow out any debris which has collected in the spark plug wells. It could fall into the hole and cause damage.

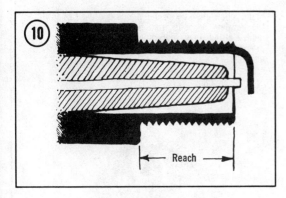

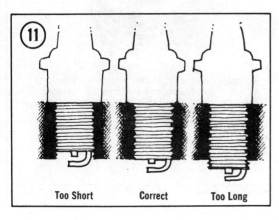

⑫

Normal plug appearance noted by the brown to grayish-tan deposits and slight electrode wear. This plug indicates the correct plug heat range and proper air fuel ratio.

Red, brown, yellow and white coatings caused by fuel and oil additives. These deposits are not harmful if they remain in a powdery form.

Carbon fouling distinguished by dry, fluffy black carbon deposits which may be caused by an over-rich air/fuel mixture, excessive hand choking, clogged air filter or excessive idling.

Shiny yellow glaze on insulator cone is caused when the powdery deposits from fuel and oil additives melt. Melting occurs during hard acceleration after prolonged idling. This glaze conducts electricity and shorts out the plug.

Oil fouling indicated by wet, oily deposits caused by oil pumping past worn rings or down the intake valve guides. A hotter plug temporarily reduces oil deposits, but a plug that is too hot leads to pre-ignition and possible engine damage.

Overheated plug indicated by burned or blistered insulator tip and badly worn electrodes. This condition may be caused by pre-ignition, cooling system defects, lean air/fuel ratios, low octane fuel or over advanced ignition timing.

Spark plug condition photos courtesy of AC Spark Plug Division, General Motors Corporation.

Table 3 SPARK PLUG GAP

| Model | Spark Plug Gap | |
	Inches	Millimeters
250-350	0.028-0.032	0.70-0.80

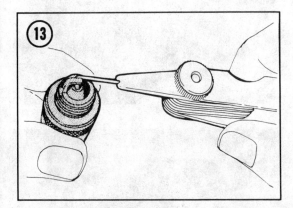

2. Gently remove the spark plug leads by pulling up and out on the cap. Do not jerk or pull on the wire itself.

3. Apply penetrating oil to the base of the plug and allow it to work into the threads.

4. Back out the plugs with a socket that has a rubber insert designed to grip the insulator. Be careful not to drop the plugs where they could become lodged.

NOTE: *Be sure that you remember which cylinder each spark plug came out of. The condition of the spark plug is an indication of engine condition and can warn of developing trouble that can be isolated by cylinder (refer to* **Figure 12**).

5. Remove the spark plug gaskets from the spark plug holes. Clean the seating area after removal, being careful that dirt does not drop into the spark plug hole.

6. Remove grease and dirt from the insulator with a clean rag. Inspect the insulator and body of each spark plug for signs of cracks and chips. Replace if defective.

NOTE: *If one plug is found unsatisfactory, replace both of them.*

7. Clean the tips of the plugs with a sandblasting machine (some gas stations have them) or a wire brush and solvent.

8. File the center electrode flat. Clean and file all surfaces of the outer electrode. All surfaces should be clean, flat, and smooth.

9. Use a round feeler gauge and adjust the clearance between the electrodes as specified in **Table 3**. See **Figure 13**.

CAUTION
Do not bend the inner electrode or damage to the insulator may result.

10. Use a new gasket if the old plugs are to be reused after cleaning. Apply a dab of graphite to the spark plug threads to simplify future removal.

11. Thread the plugs into the spark plug holes finger-tight, then tighten ¼-turn more with a wrench. Further tightening will flatten the gasket and cause binding. (If a torque wrench is available, tighten spark plugs to 15 ft.-lb.)

Breaker Points

Normal use of a motorcycle causes the breaker points to burn and pit gradually. If they are not pitted too badly, they can be dressed with a few strokes of a clean point file or Flex-stone.

CAUTION
Do not use emery cloth or sandpaper to dress the points as particles can remain on the points and cause arcing and burning.

If a few strokes of the file do not smooth the points completely, replace them.

Oil or dirt may get on the points, resulting in poor performance or even premature failure. Common causes for this condition are defective oil seals, improper or excessive breaker cam lubrication, or lack of care when the breaker point cover is removed.

Points should be cleaned and regapped every 1,500-2,000 miles (2,000-3,000 kilometers). To clean the points, first dress them lightly with a clean point file, then remove all residue with lacquer thinner. Close the points on a piece of clean white paper (such as a business card). Continue to pull the card through the closed points until no discoloration or residue remains on the card. Finally, rotate the engine and observe the points as they open and close. If they do not meet squarely, replace them.

To adjust the points, proceed as follows.

1. Remove breaker point cover (**Figure 14**).

2. Remove the alternator cover (**Figure 15**) and turn engine over until one set of points is open to the maximum gap.

3. Measure the breaker point gap with a feeler gauge (**Figure 16**). Point gap should be 0.012-0.016 in. (0.30-0.40mm). If so, go on to Step 7. If adjustment is necessary, continue with Steps 4 through 9.

4. Slightly loosen breaker points retaining screws (A). Refer to **Figure 17**.

5. Insert a screwdriver into pry slots (B), then move the stationary contact so that point gap is 0.014 in. (0.35mm) as shown in **Figure 17**.

6. Tighten both retaining screws, then check gap again. Readjust if necessary.

7. Repeat Steps 2 through 6 on remaining set of points.

8. Wipe the breaker cam clean, then apply a very small quantity of breaker cam lubricant. Apply just enough to create an oil film on the cam; more may cause point failure. This lubricant is sold at any auto parts store.

9. Adjust ignition timing (refer to *Ignition Timing*, following section).

To replace breaker points, disconnect wire which is attached to the movable contact, then remove both retaining screws. Be sure to adjust point gap and ignition timing after installation.

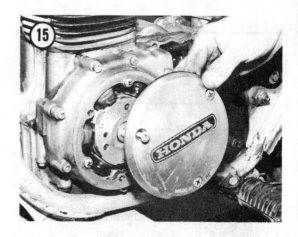

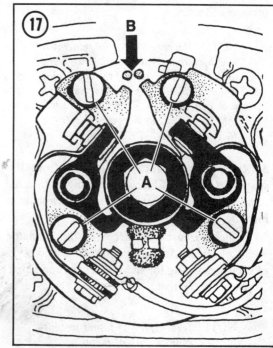

Ignition Timing

Any change in breaker point gap, either from normal wear or from breaker point service, affects ignition timing. If spark plugs fire too early, severe engine damage may result. Overheating and loss of power will occur if the spark occurs too late.

1. Remove the breaker point cover and alternator cover (**Figure 14** and **Figure 15**).

2. Place a wrench on the alternator rotor bolt and turn the engine over until the LF mark on the alternator rotor aligns with the index pointer (**Figure 18**).

3. Connect a timing tester to the left-hand breaker point terminal and a good ground (follow the manufacturer's hook-up instructions). If no timing tester is available, make up a test lamp as shown in **Figure 19**.

4. Loosen both of the left-hand points' base plate retaining screws (A, **Figure 20**) just enough so that the base plate can be moved slightly.

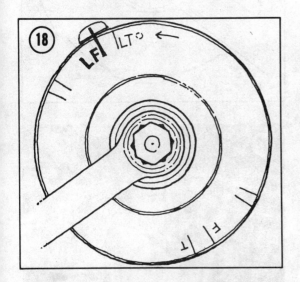

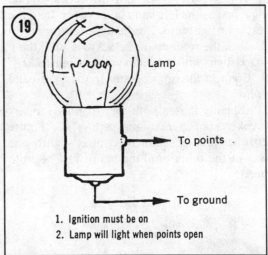

1. Ignition must be on
2. Lamp will light when points open

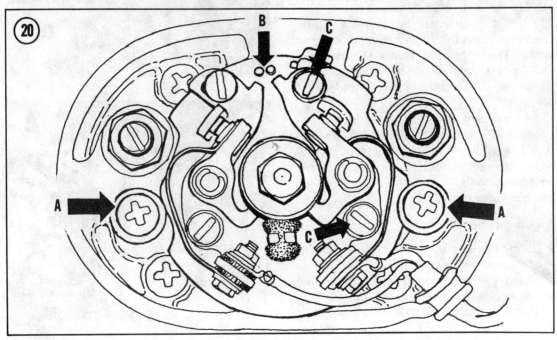

5. Insert a screwdriver in the pry slots (B, **Figure 20**) and rotate the base plate until the left-hand points just begin to open. (If a test lamp is used to determine point opening, be sure that the ignition switch in ON.) The test lamp will light exactly at the moment that the LF mark on the alternator rotor aligns with the index pointer, if the ignition timing is correct.

6. Tighten both base plate retaining screws (refer to A, **Figure 20**).

7. Recheck adjustment by turning the rotor clockwise slightly, then counterclockwise slowly. The LF mark and the index should align just as the left-hand points open (and the test lamp lights up). Readjust if necessary.

8. Turn the rotor counterclockwise until the F mark aligns with the index mark (**Figure 21**).

9. Connect the timing tester to the right-hand points.

10. Slightly loosen both right-hand stationary breaker contact retaining screws (C, **Figure 20**) then pry the stationary contact slightly one way or the other until the points just begin to open.

NOTE
The point gap will change slightly; this is normal.

11. Tighten both retaining screws (C).

12. Recheck adjustment by turning the rotor clockwise slightly, then counterclockwise slowly. The right-hand points should open, and the test lamp should light, just as the F mark and the index align. Readjust if necessary.

13. After timing is correct the point gap still should be within the 0.012-0.016 in. (0.6-0.7mm) limits. If not, reset point gap and repeat this procedure. If the point gap cannot be adjusted within these limits, replace the breaker point assemblies.

Air Cleaner Service

During the tune-up the air cleaner element should be cleaned or replaced.

1. Remove the clamps and retaining nuts and lift the air cleaner off (**Figures 22 and 23**).

2. Remove the element and tap it gently against the palm of your hand to dislodge dirt

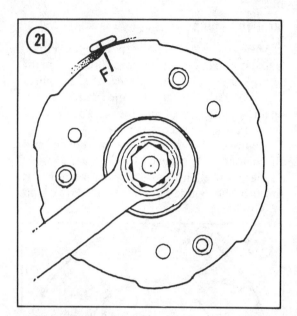

from the outside. Then blow compressed air gently from the inside. Replace a damaged element, or one that is too dirty to clean satisfactorily.

3. Install by reversing the preceding steps.

Carburetor Adjustment (C.V.Type)

1. Start the engine and allow it to warm to operating temperature.
2. Adjust each idle speed screw so that the engine idles at 1,000-1,200 rpm (**Figure 24**).
3. Place one hand behind each muffler and adjust idle speed screw (**Figure 24**) until exhaust pressure from each muffler is equal.
4. Turn left cylinder idle mixture screw (**Figure 25**) in either direction, slowly, until engine idle speed is at its maximum.

5. Repeat Step 4 for the right cylinder.
6. Check exhaust pressure from each cylinder (as in Step 3) and adjust either idle speed screw necessary to equalize pressures.
7. Turn each idle speed screw an equal amount to obtain 1,000-1,200 rpm idle speed.
8. Synchronize both carburetors (refer to last procedure, this section).

Carburetor Adjustment/ Slide Valve Type

1. Start engine and allow to warm to operating temperature, then shut it off.
2. Turn each idle mixture screw in until it seats lightly, then back out each one 1-1/4 turns (**Figure 26**).
3. Start the engine. Adjust each idle speed screw so that the engine idles at 1,00-1,200 rpm (**Figure 27**).
4. Place one hand behind each muffler and adjust idle speed screw (refer to **Figure 27**) until exhaust pressure from each muffler is equal.
5. Turn left cylinder idle mixture screw in either direction, slowly, until engine idle speed is at its maximum.
6. Repeat Step 5 for the right cylinder.
7. Check exhaust pressure from each cylinder (as in Step 4) and adjust either idle speed screw necessary to equalize pressures.
8. Turn each idle speed screw an equal amount to obtain 1,000-1,200 rpm idle speed.
9. Synchronize both carburetors (refer to last procedure, this section).

If the preceding procedure does not work well, due to both carburetors being too far out of adjustment, use the following procedure:
1. Turn the idle mixture screw on each carburetor in until it seats lightly, then back out 1-1/4 turns (refer to **Figure 26**).
2. Start the engine, then ride the bike long enough to warm it thoroughly.
3. Stop the engine and disconnect either spark plug lead.
4. Restart the engine on one cylinder. Turn the idle speed screw on the "working" carburetor in enough to keep the engine running (refer to **Figure 27**).
5. Turn the idle speed screw out until the engine runs slower and begins to falter.

6. Turn the idle mixture screw in or out to make the engine run smoothly. Note the speed indicated by the tachometer.

7. Repeat Steps 5 and 6 to achieve the lowest possible stable idle speed.

8. Stop the engine, then reconnect the spark plug lead that was disconnected.

9. Repeat Steps 3 through 8 for the other cylinder, matching the engine speed with that observed in Step 6.

10. Start the engine, then turn each idle speed screw an equal amount until the engine idles at 1,000-1,200 rpm.

11. Place one hand behind each muffler and check that the exhaust pressures are equal. If not, turn either idle speed screw in or out until they are equal.

12. Adjust carburetor synchronization (see following procedure).

Carburetor Synchronization (C.V. Type)

To synchronize the carburetors, proceed as follows:

1. Twist the throttle grip and see if both throttle valves move at the same time.

> *NOTE*
> *Place a hand under the carburetor and note the movement of the throttle levers. They should start to move at the same time.*

2. If adjustment is necessary, loosen the throttle cable locknut at the carburetors and adjust the cable adjuster bolt. Tighten the locknut.

Carburetor Synchronization (Slide Type)

To synchronize the carburetors, proceed as follows:

1. Twist the throttle grip (**Figure 28**) and see if both throttle slides begin to move at the same time.

2. If throttle slides need adjusting, turn the cable adjuster at the top of either carburetor until the slides move together perfectly (**Figure 29**).

> *NOTE*
> *A small mirror may be helpful during this check.*

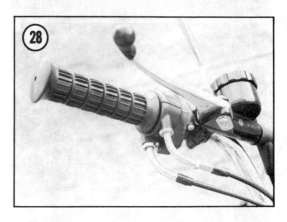

CLUTCH ADJUSTMENT

Adjust the clutch at intervals of 1,000-mile (1,500-kilometer), or whenever necessary.

1. Refer to **Figure 30**. Loosen locknut, then turn cable adjuster until cable is all the way into the clutch lever bracket.

2. Refer to **Figure 31**. Loosen locknut, then

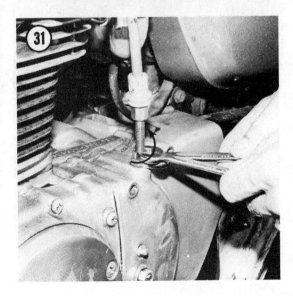

turn lower cable adjuster in direction indicated to fully loosen the cable.

3. Refer to **Figure 32**. Loosen locknut, then turn adjuster screw counterclockwise until it meets resistance. From this point on, turn it clockwise 1/4 turn. Tighten the locknut.

4. Refer to **Figure 31**. Turn lower cable adjuster so that there is approximately 3/4 in. (20mm) of free play at the clutch hand lever, then tighten the lower cable adjuster locknut.

5. Tighten upper cable adjuster locknut. Minor adjustments can then be made at the upper cable adjuster.

BRAKES

Adjust the drum brakes every 1,000 miles (1,500 kilometers), or whenever necessary. All models covered in this manual have a drum or disc type front brake and a drum type rear brake.

Front (Drum) Brake Adjustment

Refer to **Figure 33** for this procedure.

1. Support the motorcycle so that its front wheel is free to turn.

2. Loosen the cable locknut.

3. Turn the cable adjusting nut to obtain 5/8 to 1-1/4 in. (15-30mm) free play at the tip of the brake lever.

4. Tighten the locknut.

Front (Disc) Brake Adjustment

The front disc brake is self adjusting and needs no periodic maintenance other than brake pad replacement. When brake pads are replaced there is a one time adjustment required on the caliper assembly. This is covered in Chapter Seven.

Rear Brake Adjustment

The rear brake is operated by a rod. Simply turn the adjusting nut (**Figure 34**) until the rear brake pedal has approximately 3/4 to 1-1/4 in. (20-30mm) of free play (**Figure 35**).

Disc Brake Fluid Level

1. Every 1,000 miles (1,500 kilometers), remove the reservoir cap, washer and diaphragm.
2. The fluid level in the reservoir should be up to the upper level line (**Figure 36**). Correct the level by adding fresh brake fluid.

> *NOTE*
> *Use brake fluid clearly marked DOT 3 only. Others may vaporize and cause brake failure.*

> *CAUTION*
> *Be careful not to spill brake fluid on painted or plated surfaces as it will destroy the surface. Wash immediately with soapy water and thoroughly rinse it off.*

3. Reinstall the washer, diaphragm and reservoir cap. Make sure the cap is screwed on tightly.

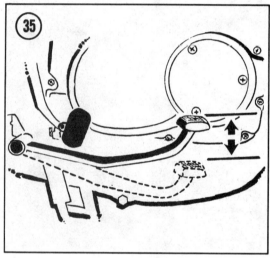

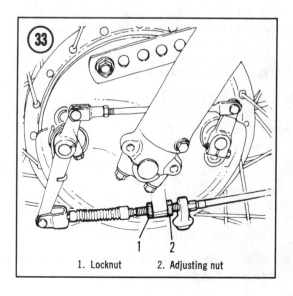

1. Locknut   2. Adjusting nut

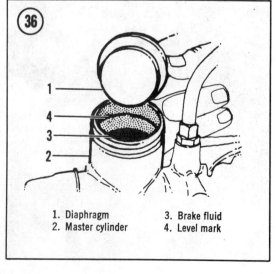

1. Diaphragm   3. Brake fluid
2. Master cylinder   4. Level mark

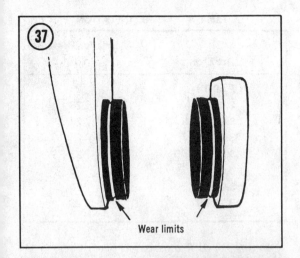

Wear limits

Disc Brake Lines

Check brake lines between the master cylinder and the brake caliper. If there is any leakage, tighten the connection and bleed the brakes as described under *Bleeding the System* in Chapter Seven. If this does not stop the leak, or the line is obviously damaged, checked, or chafed, replace the line and bleed the brake.

Disc Brake Pad Wear

Inspect the brake pads for excessive or uneven wear. If the pads are worn to the red line (**Figure 37**), they must be replaced. Refer to Chapter Seven for replacement procedures.

> *NOTE*
> *Always replace both pads at the same time.*

STEERING STEM BEARINGS

Check steering bearings for looseness or binding. Refer to Chapter Seven, *Steering Stem* section, for repair procedures.

Adjustment

1. Remove steering stem nut (**Figure 38**).
2. Loosen pinch bolt. Then tighten or loosen the ring nut by tapping it gently with a suitable drift until the steering stem turns freely throughout its full travel without excessive looseness or binding (**Figure 39**). Tighten the pinch bolt securely.
3. Tighten the steering stem nut securely (refer to **Figure 38**).

WHEELS AND TIRES

Check wheels for bent rims and loose or missing spokes. Complete wheel inspection and service procedures are detailed in Chapter Seven, *Wheels* section.

Check tires for worn treads, cuts, and proper inflation. Refer to **Table 4**.

BATTERY

The battery should always be clean and the cells filled (but not overfilled) with distilled water. Most batteries are marked with electrolyte level limit lines. Always maintain the fluid level between these two lines. (Distilled water is available at most supermarkets.)

Overfilling leads to loss of electrolyte, resulting in poor battery performance, short life, and excessive corrosion. Never allow the electrolyte level to fall below the top of the battery plates, as the plates could become permanently damaged due to contact with the air.

Excessive battery water consumption is an indication that the battery is being overcharged. The two most common causes of overcharging are high battery temperature or high voltage regulator setting.

WARNING
When working with batteries, use extreme care to avoid spilling or splashing electrolyte. This electrolyte is sulfuric acid, which can destroy clothing and cause serious chemical burns. Neutralize spilled battery acid immediately with a solution of baking soda and water, then flush away with clean water.

Safety glasses should be worn when working near a battery, to avoid having electrolyte splashed in the eyes. If electrolyte comes in contact with the eyes, force the eyes open and flood with cool, clean water for about 5 minutes, and call a physician immediately.

Battery Charging

WARNING
When batteries are being charged, highly explosive gas forms in each cell. Some of this gas escapes through the filler openings and may form an explosive atmosphere around the battery (which may last for several hours). Keep sparks, open flames, or lighted cigarettes away from a battery under charge, or in a room where one has been recently charged. A common cause of battery explosions is the disconnection of a live circuit at a battery terminal (a spark almost always occurs under these

Table 4 TIRE INFLATION	
Tire Size	Inflation Pressure (psi)
2.50-18	23
2.75-18	23
3.00-18	23
3.25-18	23
3.50-18	23
4.00-18	23
3.00-19	23
3.25-19	23

conditions). To avoid this, be sure that the power switch is off before making or breaking connections. (Poor connections are also a common cause of electrical arcs which cause explosions.)

Motorcycle batteries are not designed for high charge or discharge rates. For this reason, it is recommended that a motorcycle battery be charged at a rate not exceeding 10% of its ampere-hour capacity.

Example: Do not exceed 0.5 ampere charging rate for a 5 ampere-hour battery, or 1.5 amperes for a 15 ampere-hour battery.

This charge rate should continue for 10 hours if the battery is completely discharged, or until specific gravity of each cell is up to 1.260-1.280, corrected for temperature. If, after prolonged charging, specific gravity of one or more cells does not come up to at least 1.230, the battery will not perform as well as it should, but it may continue to provide satisfactory service for a time.

Some temperature rise is normal as a battery is being charged. Do not allow electrolyte temperature to exceed 110°F. Should temperature reach that figure, disconnect charging until the battery cools, then resume charging at a lower rate.

Testing State of Charge

Place the tube of a hydrometer into the filler opening and draw in just enough electrolyte to lift the float (**Figure 40**). Hold the instrument in a vertical position and read specific gravity on the scale, where the float stem emerges from the electrolyte.

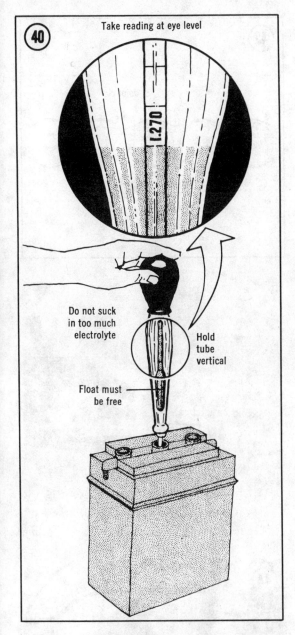

40

Take reading at eye level

1.270

Do not suck
in too much
electrolyte

Hold
tube
vertical

Float must
be free

Specific gravity of the electrolyte varies with temperature, so it is necessary to apply a temperature correction to the reading so obtained. For each 10 degress that battery temperature exceeds 80°F, add 0.004 to the indicated specific gravity. Likewise, subtract 0.004 from the indicated value for each 10° that battery temperature is below 80°F.

Repeat this measurement for each battery cell. If there is more than 0.050 difference (50 points) between cells, battery condition is questionable.

State of charge may be determined from **Figure 41**.

Do not measure specific gravity immediately after adding water. Ride the machine a few miles to ensure thorough mixture of the electrolyte.

It is most important to maintain batteries fully charged during cold weather. A fully charged battery freezes at a much lower temperature than one which is partially discharged. Freezing temperature depends on specific gravity. Refer to **Table 5**.

Battery Cables

Keep battery cables tight and clean (free of corrosion, grease, etc.). If cables are corroded, disconnect them and clean them separately with a wire brush and a baking soda and water solution. After cleaning, apply a thin coating of petroleum jelly to the battery terminals before installing the cables. After connecting the cables, apply a light coating to the connection. This procedure will help to prevent future corrosion.

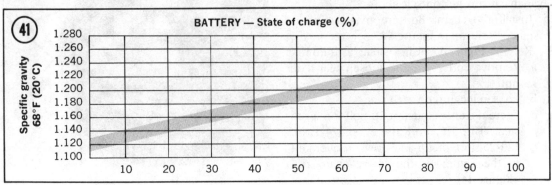

41

BATTERY — State of charge (%)

Specific gravity
68°F (20°C)

1.280
1.260
1.240
1.220
1.200
1.180
1.160
1.140
1.120
1.100

10 20 30 40 50 60 70 80 90 100

Table 5   SPECIFIC GRAVITY/FREEZING TEMPERATURE

Specific Gravity	Freezing Temperature Degrees F
1.100	18
1.120	13
1.140	8
1.160	1
1.180	—6
1.200	—17
1.220	—31
1.240	—50
1.260	—75
1.280	—92

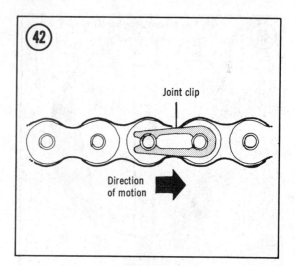

DRIVE CHAIN

Clean, lubricate, and adjust the drive chain every 1,000 miles (1,500 kilometers), or whenever necessary. The drive chain becomes worn after prolonged use. Wear in pins, bushings, and rollers cause chain stretch. Sliding action between roller surfaces and sprocket teeth also contribute to wear.

Cleaning and Adjustment

1. Disconnect the master link (**Figure 42**) and remove chain.
2. Clean chain thoroughly with solvent.
3. Rinse chain with clean solvent, then blow dry with compressed air.
4. Examine chain carefully for wear or damage. Replace if there is any doubt as to its condition. If chain is okay, lubricate by soaking in oil, or any of the special chain lubricants available in any motorcycle shop.
5. Install the chain. Be sure master link is installed as shown in **Figure 42**.
6. Refer to **Figure 43**. Adjust chain as follows:
   a. Remove cotter pin and loosen rear axle nut.
   b. Loosen locknut on each side.
   c. There is one adjustment bolt on each side. Turn it until there is 3/4-1 in. (20-25mm) of up-and-down movement in the center of the lower chain run (**Figure 44**).

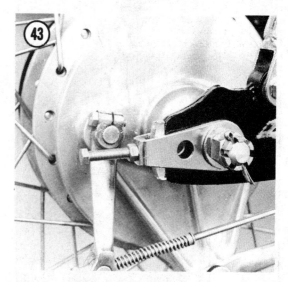

d. Be sure that the reference marks on the swinging arm and the index mark on the chain adjuster (refer to **Figure 43**) are in the same relative positions on each side.

7. Tighten the rear axle nut, then install a new cotter pin (refer to **Figure 43**).

8. Adjust the rear brake (refer to *Brakes* section, this chapter).

FORK OIL

Replacement

Replace the fork oil every 3,000 miles (4,500 kilometers), as follows:

1. Place a pan under each fork leg, then remove drain plug at lower end of each fork leg (**Figure 45**). Allow oil to drain pan into pan.

NOTE
To aid in removing all of the oil, push down on the forks several times to force oil out.

2. Install drain plugs, then remove upper fork bolts (**Figure 46**). Pour fresh fork oil into forks (refer to **Table 6** for fork oil quantities).

3. Install upper fork bolts.

OIL AND OIL FILTER

Probably the single most important maintenance item which contributes to long engine life is that of regular oil changes. Engine oil becomes contaminated with products of combustion, condensation, and dirt. Some of these contaminants react with oil, forming acids which attack vital engine components, and thereby result in premature wear.

To change engine oil, ride the bike until it is thoroughly warm, then place a pan under the engine and remove the engine oil drain plug (**Figure 47**). Allow the oil to drain thoroughly (it may help to rock the motorcycle from side to side, and also forward and backward, to get as much oil out as possible).

Install the engine oil drain plug and refill with fresh engine oil. Refer to **Table 7** and **Table 8** for specifications.

Be sure to check for leaks after the oil change is completed.

Maintain the engine oil level between both level marks on the dipstick (**Figure 48**).

NOTE
The dipstick should not be screwed into the engine when checking oil level.

All models are equipped with a centrifugal oil filter which separates sludge and other foreign particles from the engine oil before it is distributed throughout the engine. To clean the filter, proceed as follows:

1. Remove the small cover on the right-hand crankcase cover (**Figure 49**).

NOTE
This procedure is shown with the right-hand crankcase cover removed for clarity. It is not necessary to remove it for this procedure.

2. Remove the internal circlip holding the oil filter cap (**Figure 50**).
3. Remove the oil filter cap (**Figure 51**).
4. Clean all sludge and foreign particles from the cap and rotor with cleaning solvent and thoroughly dry. Be careful when cleaning the rotor that the cleaning solvent does not enter into the crankcase and contaminate the engine oil. Use as little as possible and be sure to wipe all of it out.
5. Install a new O-ring seal in the cap and install it on the rotor making sure the vane on the cap is positioned into the groove on the

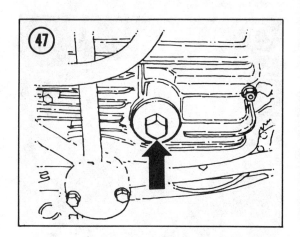

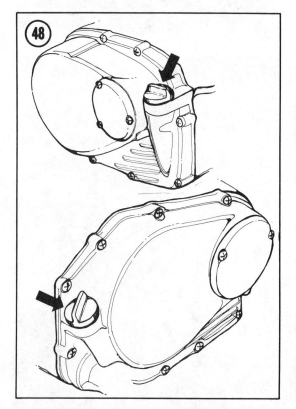

Table 6   FORK OIL CAPACITY
(AFTER DRAINING ONLY)

Model	Ounces	Cubic Centimeters
CB & CL250,350	5.9-6.3	175-185
CB & CL250,350K1,K2,K3	5.9-6.9	175-205
CB250,350K4, CL350K4, CB350G, CL350K5	3.6-3.7	105-110
SL350, SL350K1, SL350K2	5.4-5.8	160-170

Table 7   OIL GRADE

Temperature Range	Oil Grade
Below 32°F	10W, 10W-30, or 10W-40
32 to 60°F	20W, 10W-30, or 10W-40
Above 60°F	30W, 10W-30, or 10W-40

Table 8   REFILL QUANTITY

Model	Pints	Liters
250	4.2	2.0
350	4.2	2.0

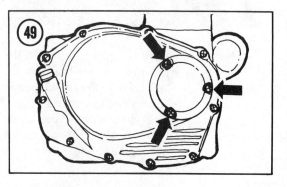

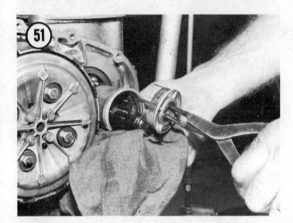

inside wall of the rotor.

6. Install a new gasket on the small cover and install it onto the crankcase cover. Be sure to install the cover with the oil filter opening located upward at the 12 o'clock position.

NOTE
Prior to installing the cover, push in on the oil guide metal and make sure it moves smoothly.

SWINGING ARM

Disassemble the swinging arm and grease its pivot shaft and bushings every 6,000 miles (9,000 kilometers). Refer to **Figure 52** for the following procedure:

1. Remove hex nut, washer, and dust seal cap.

2. Slide pivot bolt out of center collar.

3. Remove center collar; grease inside of the pivot bushing; inside and outside of center collar; and outside of pivot bolt.

4. Assemble by reversing the preceding steps.

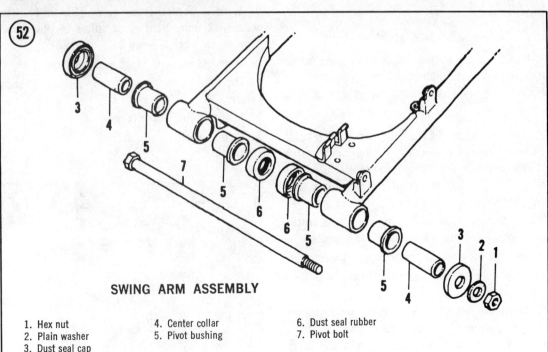

SWING ARM ASSEMBLY

1. Hex nut
2. Plain washer
3. Dust seal cap
4. Center collar
5. Pivot bushing
6. Dust seal rubber
7. Pivot bolt

CHAPTER FOUR

ENGINE, TRANSMISSION, AND CLUTCH

This chapter describes removal, disassembly, service, and reassembly of the engine, transmission, and clutch. Engine removal is not necessary for service operations on alternators, oil pumps, clutches, or shifter mechanism.

SERVICE HINTS

Experience has shown that work goes faster and easier if certain standard shop practices are observed. Some of the more important ones are listed below.

1. During engine disassembly, keep all related parts together. Reassembly will be much easier if this precaution is taken; in particular if a long period of time lapses between disassembly and reassembly.

2. All O-rings, gaskets, snap rings, and cotter pins which are removed should be replaced.

3. Be sure all parts are clean upon reassembly.

4. Lubricate all moving parts liberally before reassembly.

5. On parts attached with multiple bolts or screws, tighten those of larger diameter first. If parts are attached with inner and outer bolts or screws, tighten inner ones first.

PRELIMINARY ENGINE DISMANTLING

It is quite often easier to dismantle the engine as far as possible while it is still mounted in the frame. Proceed as follows:

1. Loosen air filter clamp screw (**Figure 1**), then remove 2 bolts holding air filter in place and remove air filter (**Figure 2**).

2. Remove exhaust pipes and mufflers.

3. Remove carburetors from cylinder heads (**Figure 3**).

4. Remove shift lever (**Figure 4**).

5. Remove the countershaft sprocket cover (**Figure 5**).

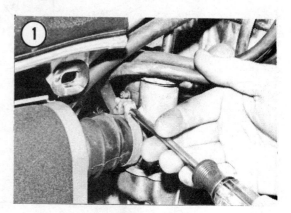

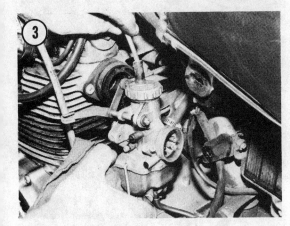

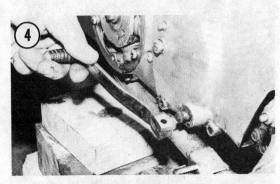

6. Remove screw holding tachometer cable and pull tachometer cable out of tachometer housing (**Figure 6**). Also, remove spark plug cable leads.

7. Remove crankcase breather hose (**Figure 7**).

8. Remove the cylinder head bracket bolts (**Figure 8**).

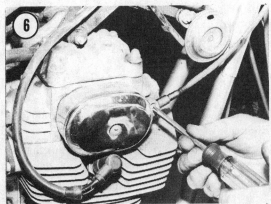

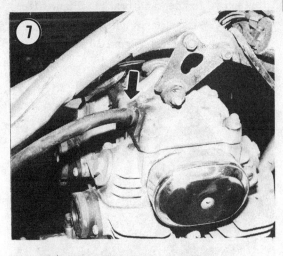

9. Remove 8 cylinder head nuts and remove cylinder head cover (**Figure 9**).

10. Remove alternator cover (**Figure 10**).

11. Remove breaker points cover, gasket, and breaker points (**Figure 11** and **Figure 12**).

12. Remove spark advance mechanism center bolt, then pull out spark advance mechanism (**Figure 13**).

13. Disengage alternator wiring connector plug (**Figure 14**).

14. Disconnect green and red wires from neutral light switch.

15. Remove alternator cover bolts and cover (**Figure 15**).

16. If work needs to be done on crankshaft, remove bolt on crankshaft rotor (**Figure 16**).

17. On right-hand side of engine, remove brake pedal (**Figure 17**).

18. Remove footpeg and bracket (**Figure 18**).

19. Remove kickstarter (**Figure 19**).

20. Remove side cover (**Figure 20**).

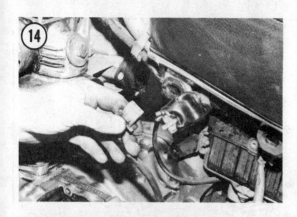

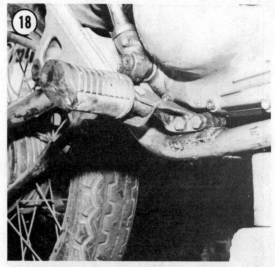

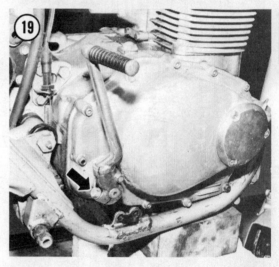

4

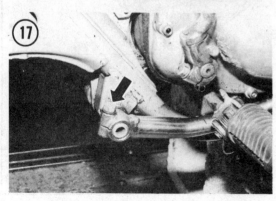

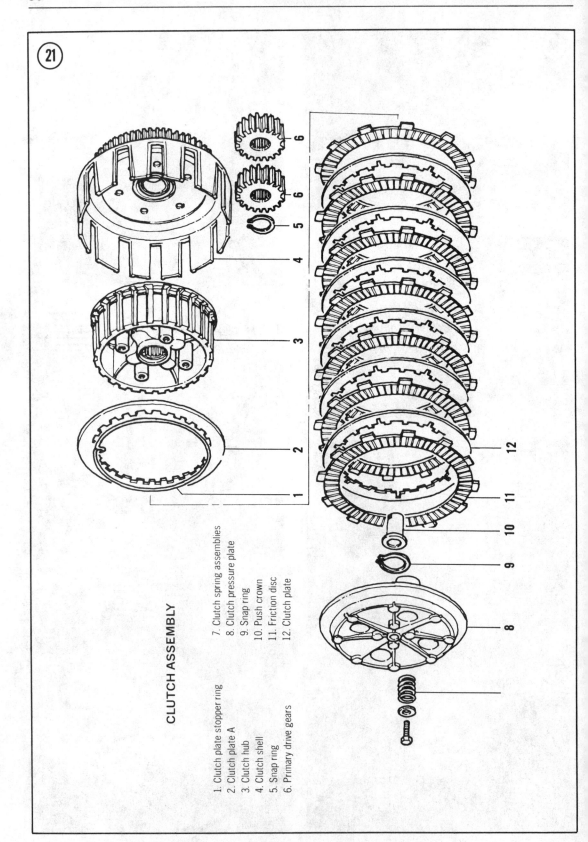

㉑

CLUTCH ASSEMBLY

1. Clutch plate stopper ring
2. Clutch plate A
3. Clutch hub
4. Clutch shell
5. Snap ring
6. Primary drive gears

7. Clutch spring assemblies
8. Clutch pressure plate
9. Snap ring
10. Push crown
11. Friction disc
12. Clutch plate

CLUTCH

On all models, the clutch is located under the right crankcase cover, and may be serviced without engine removal.

Refer to **Figure 21** for this procedure.

Removal

1. Remove both the right and left crankcase covers.

2. Remove the snap ring holding the oil filter cap in place (**Figure 22**), then remove the oil filter cap (**Figure 23**).

3. Remove the hex bolts that hold the clutch springs (**Figure 24**).

NOTE
Loosen each hex bolt a little bit at a time to equalize pressure.

4. Remove clutch springs, then remove clutch pressure plate (**Figure 25**).

5. Remove 7 friction and 6 steel plates (**Figure 26**).

6. Remove the push crown (**Figure 27**).

7. On the oil filter, bend the locking tab back, remove the locknut, and slide off the oil filter housing (**Figure 28**).

8. Remove the clutch hub snap ring (**Figure 29**).

9. Remove the clutch hub (**Figure 30**).

10. Remove the primary drive gear and thrust washer (behind the gear). See **Figure 31**.

4

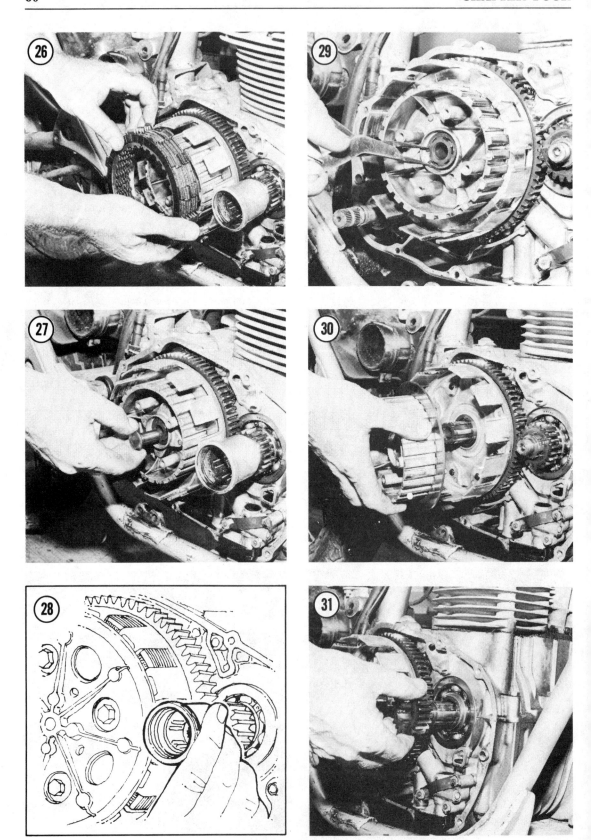

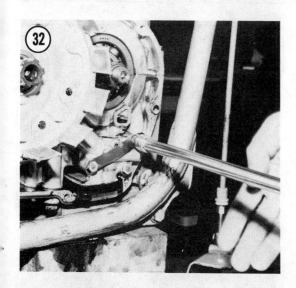

11. Remove the nuts holding the oil pump locking strap (**Figure 32**); then remove the 3 bolts holding the oil pump and remove the oil pump and clutch housing at the same time (**Figure 33**).

12. Disengage shift shaft and slide unit out (**Figure 34**).

13. Remove circlip, washer, kickstarter idle gear, and spacer (**Figure 35**).

14. Disengage the kickstarter return spring from the rib on the crankcase.

15. Remove the clutch pushrod (**Figure 36**) from the left side.

Inspection

1. Measure the thickness of each friction disc with vernier calipers (**Figure 37**). Replace all discs if any disc is worn to its limit (specified in **Table 1**).

2. Place each clutch plate on a flat surface. Using a flat feeler gauge, measure clutch plate warpage (**Figure 38**). Replace plates if any plate is warped more than 0.012 in. (0.3mm).

3. Measure free length of each clutch spring (**Figure 39**). Replace all springs as a set if any spring is shorter than its service limit (specified in **Table 2**).

Installation

1. Install spacer (**Figure 40**), then install kickstarter idle gear, washer, and circlip. Install the kickstarter return spring onto the boss on the crankcase (**Figure 41**).

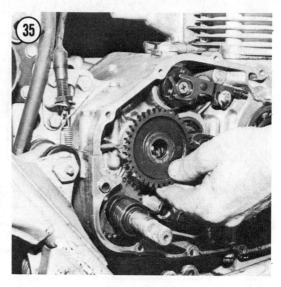

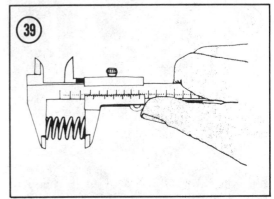

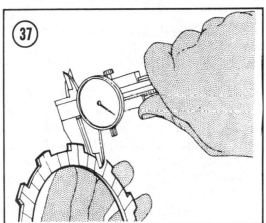

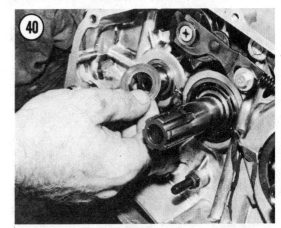

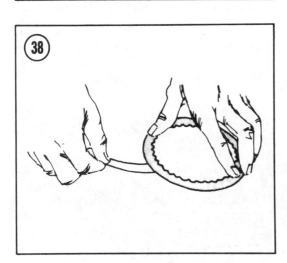

Table 1   CLUTCH DISC SPECIFICATIONS

Model	Standard Thickness		Wear Limit	
	Inches	Millimeters	Inches	Millimeters
250 and 350	0.106	2.7	0.0905	2.3

2. Install the shift shaft unit and engage it onto the shift drum (**Figure 42**).

3. Install the clutch shell and oil pump (**Figure 43**).

4. Secure the oil pump with 3 bolts, then install oil pump locking strap (**Figure 44**).

5. Install primary drive gear and thrust washer (it goes behind the gear). See **Figure 45**.

6. Install the oil filter housing, then install the flat washer, new lockwasher, and locknut (**Figure 46**). Tighten the locknut to 22 ft.-lb. (31mkg).

7. Install a new O-ring seal, then the oil filter cap (**Figure 47**).

Table 2   CLUTCH SPRING SPECIFICATIONS

Model	Standard Length		Service Limit	
	Inches	Millimeters	Inches	Millimeters
250	1.40	35.5	1.35	34.2
350	1.26	31.9	1.20	30.5

NOTE
Make sure the vane on the cap is positioned into the groove on the inside wall of the housing.

8. Install the oil filter end cap snap ring (**Figure 48**).

9. Install the thrust washer, clutch hub, and clutch hub snap ring (**Figure 49**).

10. Install the push crown (**Figure 50**).

11. Install the clutch discs in reverse order of removal (**Figure 51**). Be sure to install a friction disc first.

12. Install the clutch pressure plate cover (**Figure 52**), clutch springs (**Figure 53**), and hex bolts (**Figure 54**).

NOTE
Tighten each hex bolt that holds the clutch springs a little bit at a time to avoid distortion. Tighten hex bolts securely.

13. Install the clutch pushrod (**Figure 55**).

14. Install the right and left crankcase covers.

OIL PUMP AND FILTER

The oil pump is driven by an eccentric cam on the engine side of the clutch housing. This drives a pushrod to operate the oil pump plunger.

All models are equipped with a centrifugal oil filter which separates sludge and other foreign material from the engine oil before it is distributed throughout the engine.

Removal/Installation

Remove and install the oil pump and filter as described under *Clutch Removal and Installation* in this chapter.

Oil Pump Inspection

Refer to **Figure 56** for this procedure.

Wash all parts in cleaning solvent and thoroughly dry. Measure the outside diameter of the oil pump plunger (13) with a micrometer. Replace if it is worn to 0.627 in. (15.930mm) or smaller.

Measure the inside diameter, or bore, of the oil pump (15) with a cylinder gauge. Measure

4

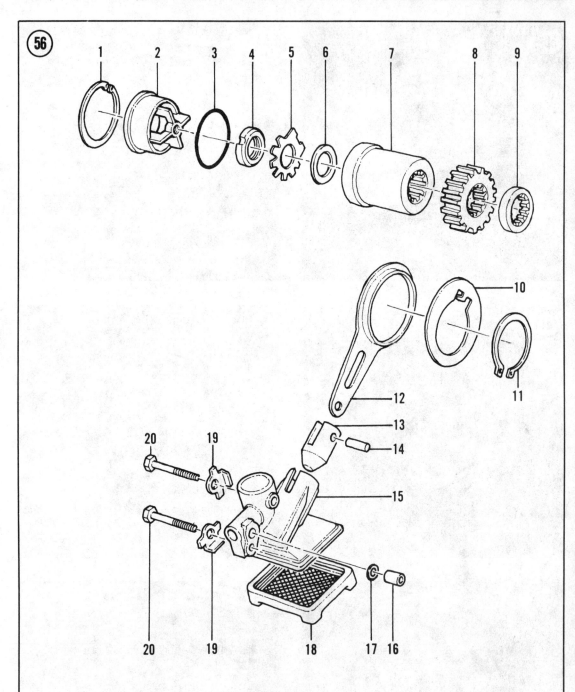

OIL PUMP AND FILTER

1. Internal circlip
2. Oil filter cap
3. O-ring
4. Locknut
5. Lockwasher
6. Filter rotor lockwasher
7. Filter rotor
8. Primary drive gear
9. Thrust washer A
10. Pump rod side washer
11. External circlip
12. Oil pump rod
13. Oil pump plunger
14. Plunger pin
15. Oil pump
16. Dowel pin A
17. O-ring
18. Oil filter screen
19. Lockwasher
20. Hex bolt

it twice at right angles to each other at the top and the bottom of the bore. Replace if it is worn to 0.634 in. (16.1mm) or greater.

Lubricate all parts prior to assembly and installation.

Oil Filter Inspection

Wash all parts in cleaning solvent and thoroughly dry. Make sure to clean out all sludge, metal particles or any foreign material that has accumulated.

Inspect all parts for wear or damage and replace as necessary. Always install a new lockwasher upon assembly.

Lubricate all parts prior to assembly and installation.

ENGINE REMOVAL

Engine removal is similar for all models listed in this manual. The following steps are set forth as a guide.

1. Warm the engine if possible, then drain engine oil into a pan.

2. Turn fuel petcock selector level to STOP then remove fuel lines from fuel petcock.

3. Remove battery cable.

4. Remove gas tank.

5. Perform all steps listed under *Preliminary Engine Dismantling* at the beginning of this chapter.

6. Remove countershaft sprocket (put bike in gear in order to aid in nut removal) and let chain dangle (**Figure 57**).

7. Remove top rear engine mounting bolt (**Figure 58**).

8. Remove lower rear engine mounting bolt (**Figure 59**).

9. Remove front lower engine mounting bolts (**Figure 60**).

10. Remove exhaust pipe mounting studs from cylinder head (place double nuts on the studs, then turn them loose with a socket and a ratchet). See **Figure 61**. This will allow the engine to be tilted forward enough to clear the frame.

11. Lift the engine out of the frame.

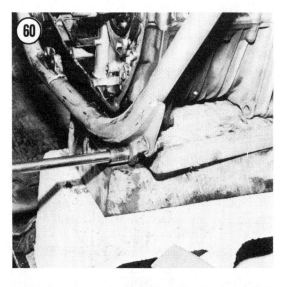

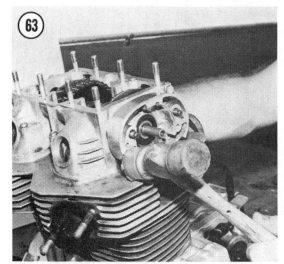

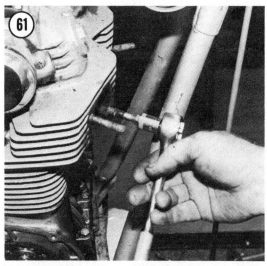

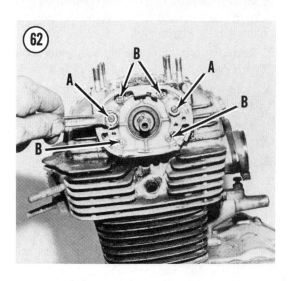

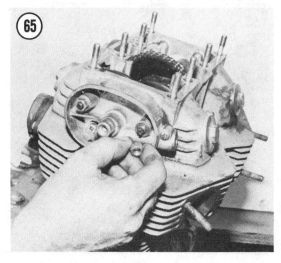

CYLINDER HEAD

Removal

1. Remove the nuts securing the rocker arm shafts (A, **Figure 62**).
2. Remove the screws (B, **Figure 62**) securing the left side cover and remove it.

> *NOTE*
> *It may be necessary to tap the side cover with a rubber or plastic mallet to break it loose (**Figure 63**).*

3. Pull out the rocker arm shafts and lift out the rocker arms (**Figure 64**).

4. Repeat Steps 1-3 on the other side of the engine (**Figure 65** and **Figure 66**).
5. Remove the cam chain tensioner (**Figure 67**).
6. Place a wrench on the alternator rotor bolt and rotate the engine until you have room to work on one of the camshaft sprocket retaining bolts. Remove that bolt, then rotate the engine until you can reach the remaining bolt and remove it. With the L mark on the cam sprocket facing upward, pull out the camshaft from the right side (**Figure 68**).
7. Remove the 4 screws holding the cam base to the cylinder head and lift off the cam base (**Figure 69**).

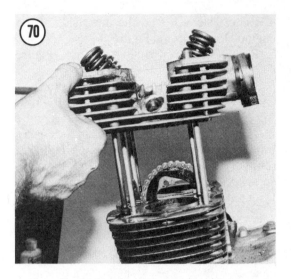

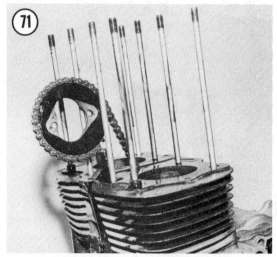

8. Remove 2 cylinder head retaining bolts, then pull off the cylinder head (**Figure 70**). These bolts are located in the spark plug wells.

> *NOTE*
> *It may be necessary to tap the cylinder head lightly with a rubber or plastic mallet; if so, take care not to break any of the cooling fins.*

9. Set the camshaft sprocket aside for now (unloop the chain from around the sprocket). Refer to **Figure 71**.

> *NOTE*
> *Tie a piece of wire to the cam chain and wrap it around any external engine component to keep from losing it down the engine.*

> *CAUTION*
> *Be careful that you do not lose the locating dowels. Discard the old O-rings and replace with new ones or oil leakage will occur.*

Inspection

1. Refer to **Figure 72**. Measure the cylinder head warpage with a straightedge and feeler gauge. Warpage must not exceed 0.002 in. (0.05mm). If clearance exceeds that value, resurface or replace the cylinder head.
2. Remove carbon from each combustion chamber with a wire brush chucked into an electric drill. (This operation is easier with valves still installed in the cylinder head.)

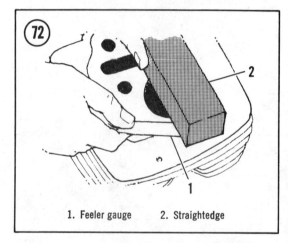

1. Feeler gauge   2. Straightedge

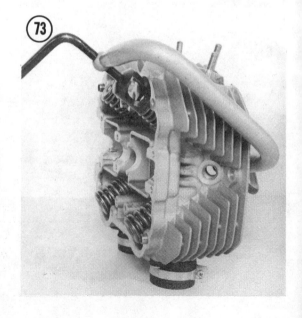

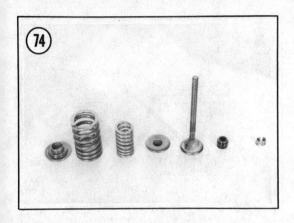

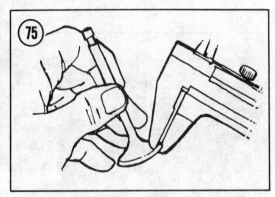

Valve Service

Valve service is best left to a machine shop which has the experience and equipment to handle small engines. Service procedures are given for those of you with the proper equipment to handle this operation.

1. Compress each valve spring and remove the valve keeper (**Figure 73**).

2. Remove the valve spring compressor, then the valve springs and valve components (refer to **Figure 74**, left to right: valve spring seat, outer spring, inner spring, top collar, valve, O-seal, and split collar).

3. Measure side clearance of each valve while it is positioned in the cylinder head, using a dial indicator. Refer to **Table 3** and replace any valve and/or its guide if clearance exceeds the service limits specified.

4. Measure valve stem diameter at 3 locations on the valve stem. Refer to **Table 4**. Replace any valve if its stem is worn to less than the service limits specified.

NOTE
When replacing valves, it is recommended that valve guides be replaced also. To do so, tap the guide from the cylinder head with a valve driving tool and a light hammer. Always install oversize guides when replacement is necessary, then ream to fit. Valve guide tools and reamers can be obtained through your Honda dealer.

5. Measure width of each valve face as shown in **Figure 75**. Refer to **Table 5**. Grind valves to service limits specified.

6. Measure free length of each valve spring as shown in **Figure 76**. Refer to **Table 6**. Replace any valve spring with a free length shorter than specified in the service limits.

Table 3   VALVE STEM CLEARANCE

| Model | Service Limit | |
	Inches	Millimeters
250 and 350		
Intake	0.0032	0.08
Exhaust	0.0035	0.09

Table 4   VALVE STEM SERVICE LIMITS

| Model | Service Limit | |
	Inches	Millimeters
250 and 350		
Intake	0.2738	6.95
Exhaust	0.2730	6.93

Table 5   VALVE FACE WIDTH

| Model | Standard Width | | Service Limit | |
	Inches	Millimeters	Inches	Millimeters
250 and 350	0.039-0.051	1.0-1.3	0.08	2.0

Table 6   VALVE SPRING FREE LENGTH

| Model | Service Limit | |
	Inches	Millimeters
250 and 350		
Outer	1.88	47.8
Inner	1.55	39.3

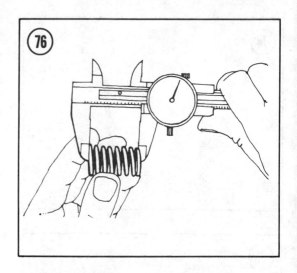

7. Install the valve seat (**Figure 77**). Then install the seal, springs, and top collar. Compress the springs with a valve spring compressor and install the keeper (**Figure 78**).

> *NOTE*
> *Install the valve springs with the narrow pitch end (end with coils close together) facing the cylinder head.*

Cylinder Head Installation

1. Clean old gasket material from cylinder head and cylinder mating surfaces, and install a new gasket (coat the cylinder base with gasket cement).

> *CAUTION*
> *Be careful that you do not lose the dowels. Be sure to discard the old O-rings and replace them with the new ones, or oil leakage will be sure to occur (**Figure 79**).*

2. Unwrap the piece of wire from around the engine component that you attached it to, to keep the chain from falling down inside the engine. Pull the chain up through the center slot in the cylinder head gasket and let it drape over the side of the engine. Set the cylinder head down over the cylinder head studs (**Figure 80**).
3. Pull the cam chain up through the head (**Figure 81**).
4. Install and tighten the 2 cylinder head mounting bolts (**Figure 82**). Tighten to 7 ft.-lb. (90 kgcm).
5. Remove the wire from the cam chain and loop the chain around the cam sprocket. Then wrap wire around chain *and* sprocket (**Figure 83**).

> *NOTE*
> *The L on the sprocket faces the left-hand side of the engine.*

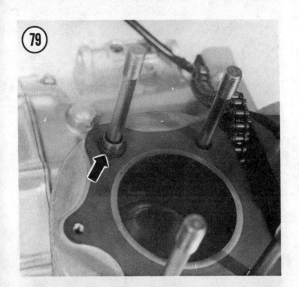

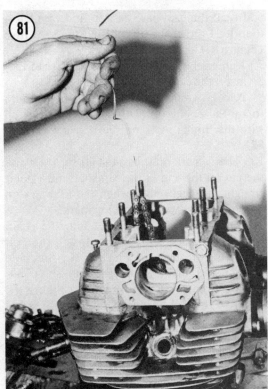

6. Install the cam base gasket, and cam base, then feed the chain up through the cam base (**Figure 84**).

7. Tighten the cam base screws (**Figure 85**).

8. Insert the camshaft (**Figure 86**).

9. Place a wrench on the alternator nut and rotate the engine until the LT mark lines up with the timing mark on the housing (**Figure 87**).

10. The L mark on the camshaft sprocket and the pin on the end of the camshaft must point straight up (**Figure 88**) when the LT mark on the rotor aligns with the timing mark.

11. Fit the camshaft sprocket into the chain with the L mark still vertical. Install the bolt which is threaded all the way in the hole nearest the L mark. Rotate the crankshaft 360° (with a wrench on the rotor). See **Figure 87**. Install the shouldered bolt (threaded partially). See **Figure 89**. Torque both bolts to 13-15 ft.-lb. (1.8-2.2 mkg).

12. Rotate the engine until the cam lobes face away from the rocker arms. Install the rocker arms by holding them in position in the head with one hand, and inserting the rocker arm shaft with the other (**Figure 90**).

13. **Figure 91** shows the rocker arms installed correctly.

> *NOTE*
> *Rotate the crankshaft through 2 complete revolutions by hand. If there is any binding at all STOP. Disassemble the cylinder head and find the problem.*

14. Install the screws securing the side covers at both ends of cam case (**Figure 92**).

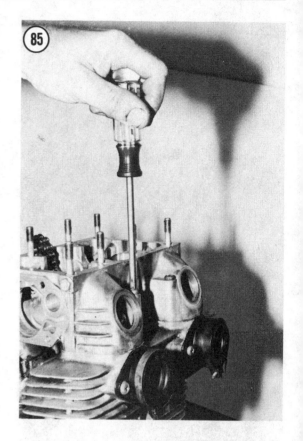

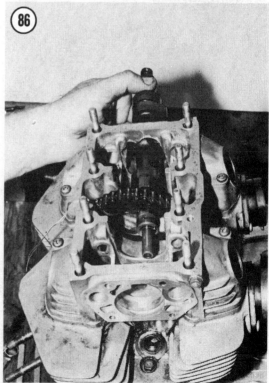

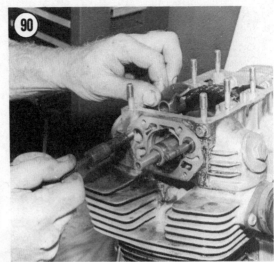

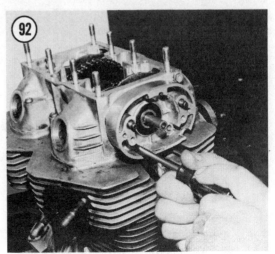

4

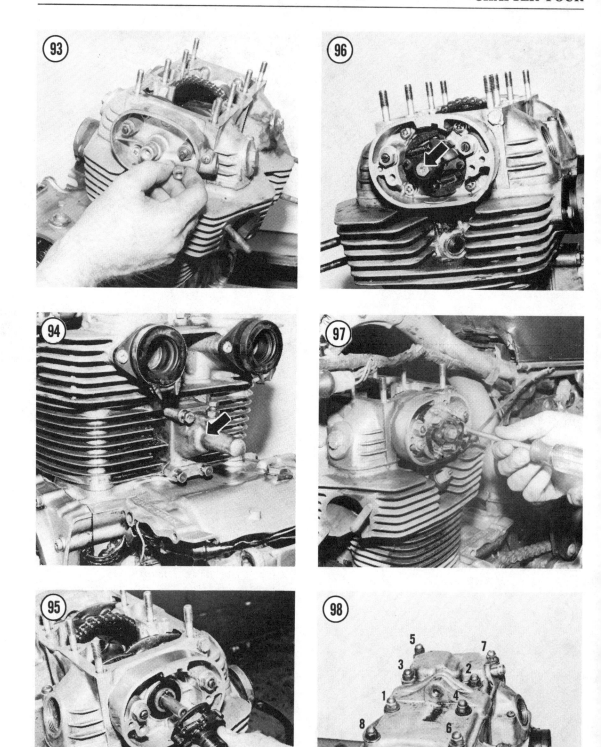

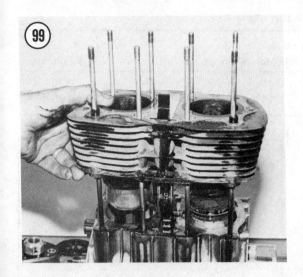

Table 7   CYLINDER WEAR LIMITS

| Model | Cylinder Wear Limit | |
	Inches	Millimeters
250	2.209	56.1
350	2.524	64.1

CYLINDERS AND PISTONS

The cylinders are of cast lightweight aluminum alloy, and have cast iron liners of sufficient thickness to permit boring and honing after long usage or piston seizure. Pistons are of lightweight aluminum alloy.

Cylinder Removal

1. Remove the cylinder head (refer to *Cylinder Head Removal*, preceding section).
2. Lift the cylinders up and off the crankcase (**Figure 99**).

NOTE
It may be necessary to tap the cylinders with a rubber or plastic mallet in order to remove them. If so, take care not to damage the cooling fins.

Checking Cylinders

Measure cylinder diameter at the top, middle, and bottom of each cylinder, using an accurate cylinder gauge. Measurements should be made both parallel and at a right angle to the crankshaft at each measurement depth. If any measurement exceeds the wear limit specified in **Table 7**, or if any 2 measurements differ by 0.002 in. (0.05mm), rebore and hone the cylinder to the next oversize. Pistons are available in oversizes of 0.25, 0.50, 0.75, and 1.00mm.

After boring and honing, the difference between the maximum and minimum measurements should not exceed 0.002 in. (0.05mm).

Piston Removal

1. Support the pistons with a piece of wood and remove the outside piston pin clip (**Figure 100**).
2. Drive the piston pin out (**Figure 101**) and remove the piston.

15. Install the nuts securing the rocker arm shafts on both ends of cam case (**Figure 93**).
16. Install cam chain tensioner (**Figure 94**).
17. Install spark advance mechanism (**Figure 95**) and secure with center bolt (**Figure 96**).

NOTE
Be sure to align the pins when installing the spark advance mechanism.

18. Install the breaker point assembly with 2 screws (**Figure 97**).

19. Install cylinder head cover and tighten nuts evenly to 14 ft.-lb. (190cmkg) in the order shown in **Figure 98**.
20. Adjust the cam chain tensioner, valves, and breaker points as described in Chapter Three.

Table 8   PISTON RING GAP

Model	Standard Value		Wear Limit	
	Inches	Millimeters	Inches	Millimeters
250	0.006	0.15	0.029	0.75
350	0.008	0.20	0.031	0.80

NOTE
If piston pin is a very tight fit, lay rags soaked in hot water around the piston. The pin will come out quite easily after a few moments. Wipe up any excess hot water with a soft, clean cloth.

Piston Ring Replacement

1. Spread the top piston ring with a thumb on each end of the ring, and remove it from the top of the piston. Take care not to scratch the piston. Repeat this procedure for each remaining ring.

2. Scrape heavy carbon deposits from the piston head (**Figure 102**). A broken hacksaw blade with its corners slightly rounded makes a good scraper.

3. Clean carbon and gum from the piston ring grooves (**Figure 103**) using a broken ring. Any deposits remaining in ring grooves will cause replacement rings to stick, thereby causing gas blow-by and loss of power.

4. Measure piston rings for wear as shown in **Figure 104**. Insert each piston ring into the cylinder to a depth of 0.2 in. (5mm). To ensure that the ring is squarely in the cylinder, push it into position with the piston head. Standard gaps and wear limits are specified in **Table 8**.

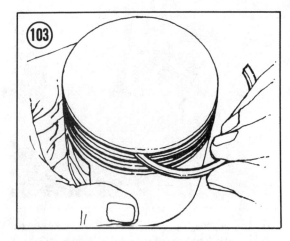

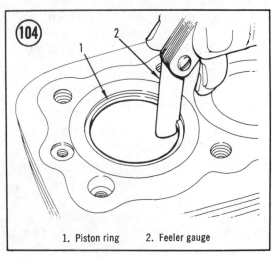

1. Piston ring   2. Feeler gauge

Table 9   PISTON RING GROOVE CLEARANCE

| | Standard Clearance | | Service Limit | |
Model	Inches	Millimeters	Inches	Millimeters
250 and 350				
Top	0.0012-0.0024	0.030-0.060	0.007	0.18
Second	0.0006-0.0018	0.015-0.045	0.006	0.16
Oil	0.0004-0.0018	0.010-0.045	0.007	0.17

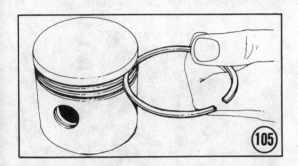

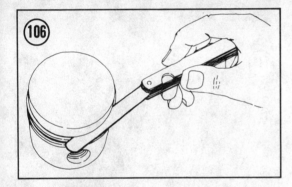

Replace all rings if any ring is worn so much that the piston ring gap exceeds the wear limit.

5. Before installing rings, check fit of each one in its groove. To do so, slip the outer surface of the ring into its groove, then roll the ring completely around the piston (**Figure 105**). If any binding occurs, determine and correct its cause before proceeding.

6. After installation, measure clearance between each ring and its groove at several places around the piston, as shown in **Figure 106**. Replace the ring and/or piston if ring groove clearance exceeds service limits specified in **Table 9**.

7. When replacing piston rings, install the lower one first. Be sure that they are installed so that all manufacturer's marks are toward the piston crown. If this precaution is not observed, oil pumping will occur. Position piston rings so that their gaps are staggered at 120-degree intervals (**Figure 107**).

Piston Clearance

Piston clearance is the difference between maximum piston diameter and minimum cylinder diameter. Measure piston diameter across the piston skirt (**Figure 108**) at right

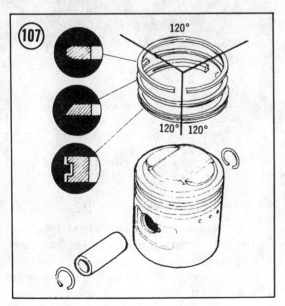

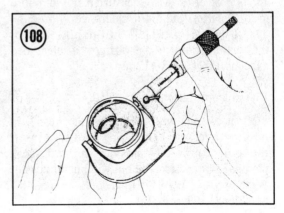

Table 10   PISTON CLEARANCE

Model	Standard Clearance		Wear Limit	
	Inches	Millimeters	Inches	Millimeters
250 and 350	0.0008-0.0020	0.02-0.05	0.008	0.20

angles to the piston pin. Standard piston clearances and wear limits are listed in **Table 10**.

A piston showing signs of seizure will result in noise, loss of power, and cylinder wall damage. If such a piston is reused without correction, another seizure will develop. To correct this condition, lightly smooth the affected area with No. 400 emery paper or a fine oilstone. Replace any piston which is deeply scratched.

Piston Pins

Measure piston pin diameter at its center and at both ends. Also measure piston pin bore in the piston. Standard clearance should be 0.0001-0.0006 in. (0.002-0.014mm). Replace the pistons and/or piston pin if clearance exceeds 0.0047 in. (0.12mm).

Piston Installation

1. Coat pistons with assembly oil and set in position over the connecting rods and insert the piston pins. (If pins go in hard, soak pistons in hot water; the pin will push in easily. Wipe excess water off with a soft, clean cloth.) See **Figure 109**.

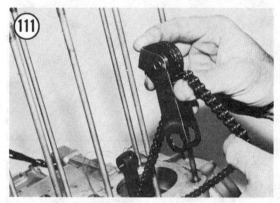

NOTE
If IN is stamped on the piston, that mark should be toward the intake valve at the rear. If an arrow is stamped on the piston, it should face the front of the engine.

2. Install new piston pin clips (refer to **Figure 100**).

Cylinder Installation

1. Coat the cylinder bore with assembly oil.
2. Insert the chain guide in the cylinder base (**Figure 110**).
3. Thread the chain through the tensioner (**Figure 111**), then position the roller and

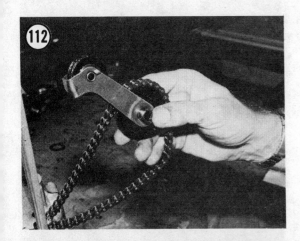

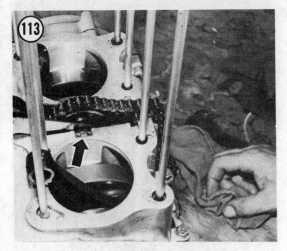

insert the pin (**Figure 112**). Position the tensioner in the crankcase and install the rubber plugs (one on each side of the tensioner). See **Figure 113**.

4. Coat the cylinder base with gasket cement, and install a new gasket.

5. Set the cylinder carefully over the studs (**Figure 114**).

CAUTION
Be sure that the cylinder locating dowels are in position.

6. Gently depress the piston rings with a screwdriver (be careful not to nick the metal). See **Figure 115**.

7. Push the cylinder firmly down onto the crankcase.

8. Install the cylinder head (refer to *Cylinder Head* section, earlier in this chapter).

CRANKCASE

Crankcases on all models split into upper and lower halves without special tools. It is necessary to split crankcase halves to service the crankshaft, transmission, internal shifter components, and kickstarter. Although details differ slightly between various models, the following service procedures are generally applicable to all models.

Disassembly

1. Remove the cylinder head, cylinder, pistons, and starter motor as outlined in previous sections.
2. Remove both right and left crankcase covers.
3. Remove the bolt securing the alternator rotor (A, **Figure 116**).
4. Screw in a flywheel puller (Honda part No. 07933-2160000 or equivalent) until it stops. Gradually tighten the puller until the rotor disengages from the crankshaft. Tap the end of the puller with a plastic mallet if the rotor will not break loose.
5. Remove the starter motor sprocket and chain (B, **Figure 116**).
6. Remove the starting sprocket retaining plate (A, **Figure 117**) and remove the starting sprocket (B, **Figure 117**).
7. Remove the clutch, oil filter, oil pump, and shift mechanism (refer to *Clutch Removal* earlier in this chapter).
8. Remove the five 8mm bolts, and eleven 6mm bolts holding both crankcases together. Gently tap on the cases with a rubber or plastic mallet and separate the 2 crankcase halves. Don't lose the 2 locating dowels.

> *CAUTION*
> *Do not pry or use any metal tool to separate the 2 crankcase halves. Mating surfaces may be damaged, resulting in an oil leak.*

Inspection

Lubricating oil passages are machined in the crankcase. Be very careful that these passages do not become clogged during service operations. If any passage is clogged, blow it out with compressed air. Examine mating surfaces of both halves for nicks or scratches which will result in oil leaks. Clean off all traces of old sealing compound.

Reassembly

1. Be sure that mating surfaces of both crankcase halves are clean.
2. Coat mating surfaces with liquid gasket compound.

> *CAUTION*
> *Do not get gasket compound on dowel pins or surfaces which do not mate.*

3. Assemble both crankcase halves and install bolts. Torque the 8mm blots to 11.5-12.2 ft.-lb. (1.6-1.7 mkg); the 6mm bolts to 5.8-6.5 ft.-lb. (0.8-0.9 mkg).

CRANKSHAFT

The crankshaft operates under conditions of high stress. Dimensional tolerances are critical. It is necessary to locate and correct crankshaft defects early to prevent more serious troubles later.

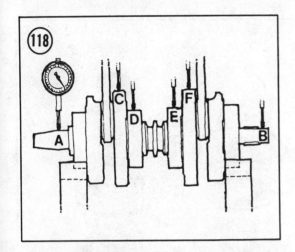

Removal

1. Split the crankcase halves (refer to *Crankcase* section, preceding).
2. Lift out the crankshaft.

Inspection

Measurement locations and support points are shown in **Figure 118**. Replace the crankshaft if runout exceeds 0.002 in. (0.05mm) at locations C, D, E, or F. Maximum runout tolerance at locations A or B is 0.006 in. (0.15mm).

Installation

1. To install the crankshaft, reverse the removal procedure.

> *CAUTION*
> *Be sure that the locating pins on each bearing engage their respective holes in the crankcase (**Figure 119**).*

2. Torque center bearing cap bolts to 15.9-17.4 ft.-lb. (220-240 cmkg). Lubricate the crankshaft bearings with the engine oil before installation.

TRANSMISSION

Removal

1. Split the crankcase and remove the crankshaft as outlined in preceding sections.
2. Lift out the main shaft and countershaft assemblies (**Figure 120**).

Countershaft
Disassembly/Inspection/Assembly

Refer to **Figure 121** for this procedure.
1. Slide off the needle bearing (2); don't lose the locating pin (1) on the needle bearing.
2. Slide off 1st gear (3) and 4th gear (4).
3. Remove the circlip and splined washer.
4. Slide off 3rd gear (5).
5. Remove the lockwasher and splined washer (on models so equipped).
6. Slide off 2nd gear (8).
7. Remove the splined washer and circlip.
8. Slide off 5th gear (9).
9. Remove the bearing (10) and oil seal if necessary.

TRANSMISSION ASSEMBLY

1. Locating pin
2. Needle bearing
3. Countershaft 1st gear
4. Countershaft 4th gear
5. Countershaft 3rd gear
6. Lockwasher
7. Splined washer
8. Countershaft 2nd gear
9. Countershaft 5th gear
10. Ball bearing
11. Countershaft
12. Oil seal
13. Drive sprocket
14. Drive sprocket fixing plate
15. Bearing set ring
16. Ball bearing
17. Main shaft
18. Main shaft 4th gear
19. Main shaft 2nd/3rd gear
20. Main shaft 5th gear
21. Locating pin
22. Needle bearing
23. Oil seal

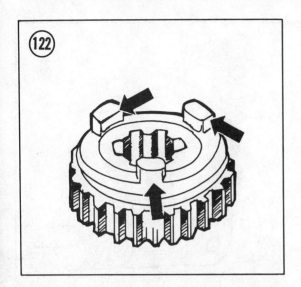

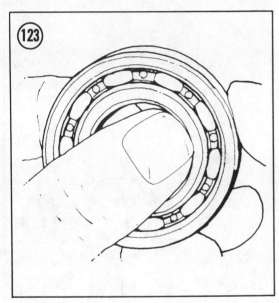

13. Check the condition of the bearing. Make sure it rotates smoothly (**Figure 123**) with no signs of wear or damage. Replace if necessary.

14. Assemble by reversing these disassembly steps. Make sure that all circlips are seated correctly in the countershaft grooves. If the oil seal was removed, replace it with a new one.

15. Make sure each gear engages properly to the adjoining gear where applicable.

**Main Shaft
Disassembly/Inspection/
Assembly**

Refer to **Figure 121** for this procedure.

1. Remove the oil seal (23) and discard it.

2. Slide off the needle bearing (22) and thrust washer. Don't lose the locating pin (21) on the needle bearing.

3. Slide off 5th gear (20).

4. Slide off the 2nd/3rd combination gear (19).

5. Remove the circlip and splined washer.

6. Slide off 4th gear (18).

7. Clean all parts in cleaning solvent and thoroughly dry.

8. Check each gear for excessive wear, burrs, pitting, or chipped or missing teeth. Make sure the lugs (**Figure 122**) on the ends of gears are in good condition.

NOTE
Defective gears should be replaced, and it is a good idea to replace the mating gear on the countershaft even though it may not show as much wear or damage.

9. Make sure that all gears slide smoothly on the main shaft splines.

10. Check the condition of the bearing (16). Make sure it rotates smoothly (**Figure 123**) with no signs of wear or damage. Replace if necessary.

11. Assemble by reversing these disassembly steps. Make sure that all circlips are seated correctly in the main shaft grooves. When installing the 2nd/3rd combination gear, slide it on with the larger diameter gear on first. Install a new oil seal.

12. Make sure each gear engages properly to the adjoining gear where applicable.

10. Clean all parts in cleaning solvent and thoroughly dry.

11. Check each gear for excessive wear, burrs, pitting, or chipped or missing teeth. Make sure the lugs (**Figure 122**) on the ends of gears are in good condition.

NOTE
Defective gears should be replaced, and it is a good idea to replace the mating gear on the main shaft even though it may not show as much wear or damage.

12. Make sure that all gears slide smoothly on the countershaft splines.

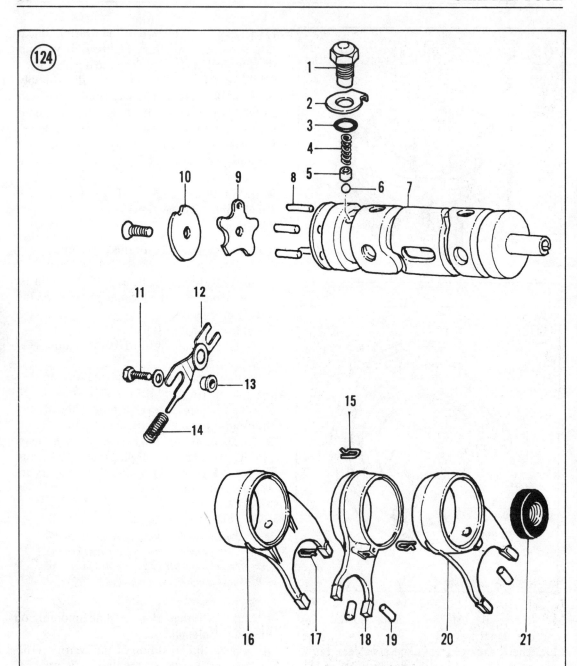

SHIFT DRUM ASSEMBLY

1. Guide screw	8. Gearshift drum pins	15. Clip
2. Lockwasher	9. Cam plate	16. Right gearshift fork
3. O-ring	10. Stopper collar	17. Clip
4. Spring	11. Bolt	18. Center gearshift fork
5. Guide screw collar	12. Shift drum stopper	19. Guide pin
6. Steel ball	13. Bushing	20. Left gearshift fork
7. Gearshift drum	14. Spring	21. Oil seal

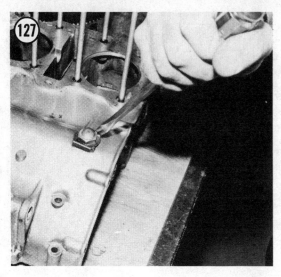

Installation

1. Install the main shaft and countershaft assemblies in the crankcase (**Figure 120**).

> *NOTE*
> *Be sure the shafts are situated over their respective locating pins in the crankcase bottom half. Make sure the set rings on the bearings are in place in the grooves in the crankcase.*

2. Install the crankshaft (refer to *Crankshaft* section, preceding) and reassemble the crankcase halves, as outlined in the *Crankcase* section, earlier in this chapter.

SHIFT CAM AND SHIFT FORKS

The shift cam and shift forks, together with the shifter mechanism, select various gear ratios within the transmission. Service is similar on all models.

Refer to **Figure 124** for this procedure.

Removal

1. Split the crankcase, and remove the crankshaft and transmission shafts as outlined previously.
2. Remove the bolt on the shift drum stopper (**Figure 125**) and lift out the shift drum stopper (**Figure 126**).
3. Remove the safety tab and loosen the bolt on the shift drum retainer (**Figure 127**). On the inside of the case, remove the bolt, spring, and ball bearing (**Figure 128**).
4. Remove neutral switch rotor (**Figure 129**).
5. Remove guide pin clips (**Figure 130**) and pull shift fork guide pins put of their recesses (**Figure 131**).

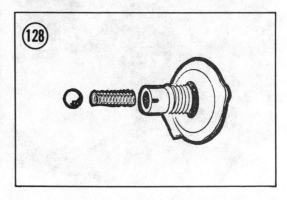

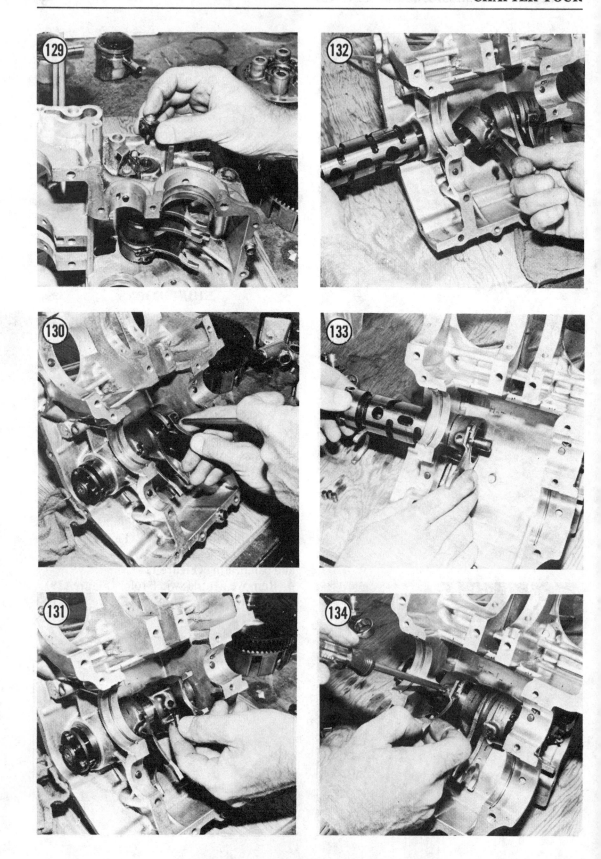

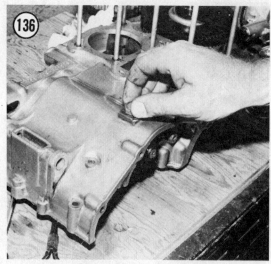

6. Slide shift drum out (hold forks in one hand) as shown in **Figure 132**.

Inspection

1. Measure clearance between each shift fork and the shift drum. Replace shift forks and/or shift drum if clearance exceeds 0.006 in. (0.15mm).

2. Examine each shift fork for bending or evidence of rubbing on one side. Measure clearance between each shift fork and the groove on its associated gear. Any clearance greater than 0.025 in. (0.6mm) should be considered excessive. Replace the shift fork and/or gear if this situation exists.

Installation

1. Install the shift drum and shift forks in the crankcase as follows:
   a. Slide shift drum into case. Slip the forks over the end of the shift drum, one at a time (**Figure 133**).
   b. Insert shift fork guide pins in their recesses (**Figure 134**).

> *NOTE*
> *The shift fork guide pins are hollow. Be sure to install them with their solid ends first.*

   c. Install guide pin clips (**Figure 135**).

2. Turn shift shaft while looking down into the bolt hole in order to locate the detent. Install the ball bearing, spring, and bolt (refer to **Figure 128**). Tighten the shift drum retaining bolt and install the safety tab (**Figure 136**).

3. Install the shift arm stopper plate in position shown in **Figure 137**. Then install bolt (**Figure 138**). Check to be sure that the shift arm stopper can be moved as shown in **Figure 139**.

4. Install the neutral switch rotor (be sure that the tab goes in the slot). See **Figure 140**.

5. Install the transmission input and output shafts, and crankshaft, as outlined previously.

6. In the other crankcase half, install kickstarter gear as shown in **Figure 141** (stop and clip facing down). Note how the anti-rattle spring is installed.

7. Install the snap ring to secure the kickstarter gear in place (**Figure 142**).

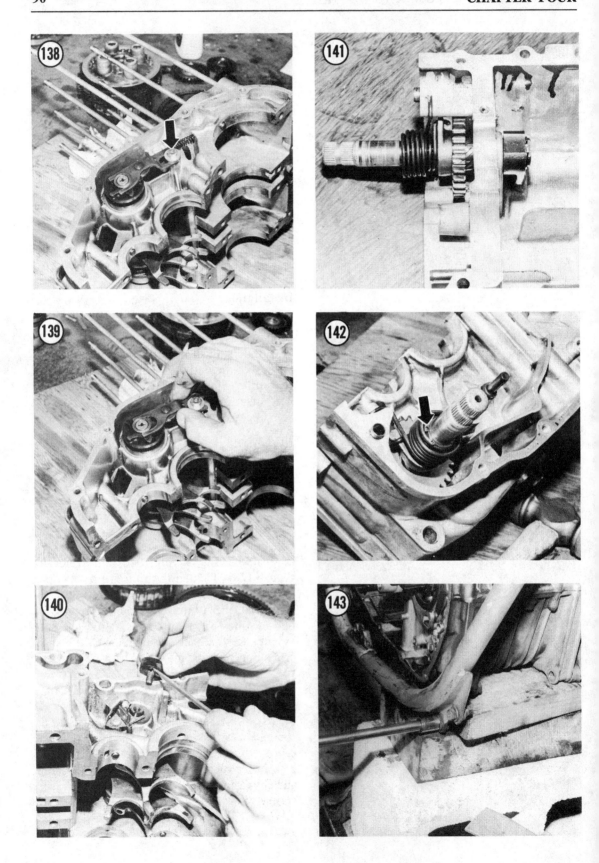

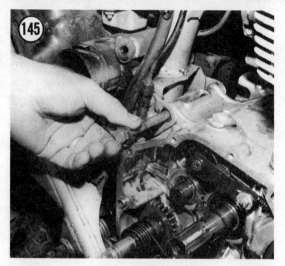

8. Reassemble the crankcase halves (refer to *Crankcase* section, earlier in this chapter).

ENGINE INSTALLATION

1. Set engine into frame.
2. Lift engine slightly, then install lower engine mounting bolts (**Figure 143**, front; **Figure 144**, rear).
3. Install top rear engine mounting bolt (**Figure 145**).
4. Install exhaust pipe mounting studs in cylinder head, using double nuts, a socket, and a ratchet, as shown in **Figure 146**.
5. Install countershaft sprocket (put bike in gear in order to aid in nut tightening). Refer to **Figure 147**.
6. Install gas tank.
7. Install battery cable.
8. Connect fuel lines to fuel petcock.
9. Install the crankcase drain plug.
10. Install side cover (**Figure 148**).
11. Install kickstarter (**Figure 149**).
12. Install footpeg and bracket (**Figure 150**).
13. Install brake pedal (**Figure 151**).
14. Install the crankshaft rotor and bolt (**Figure 152**).
15. Install the alternator cover and bolts (**Figure 153**).
16. Connect green and red wires from neutral light switch.
17. Connect alternator wiring connector plug (**Figure 154**).

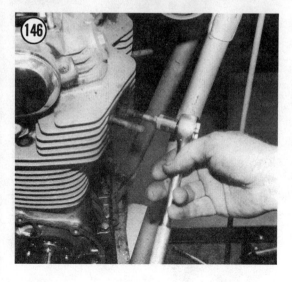

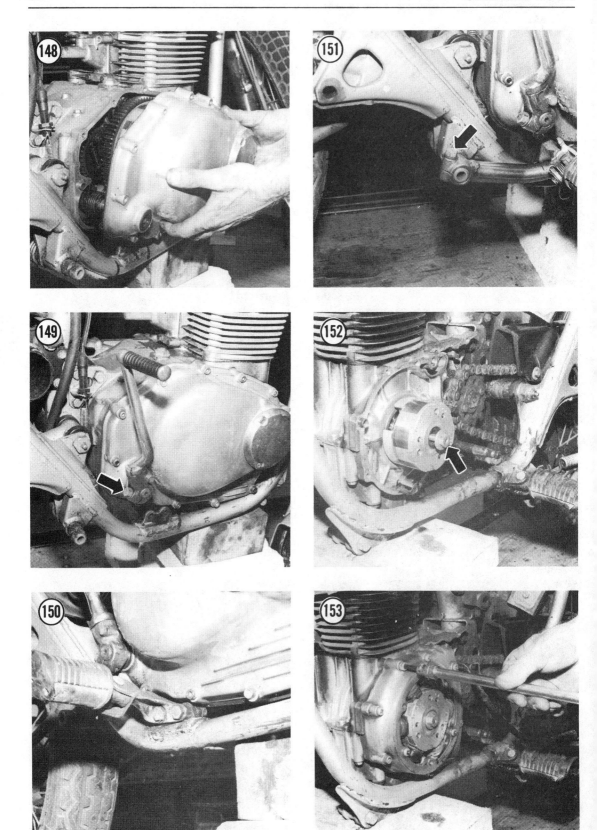

18. Install spark advance mechanism and secure with center bolt (**Figure 155**).
19. Install breaker points, gasket, and breaker points cover (**Figure 156** and **Figure 157**).
20. Install alternator cover (**Figure 158**).
21. Install the cylinder head bracket bolts (**Figure 159**).
22. Install the crankcase breather hose (**Figure 160**).
23. Install spark plug cable leads. Then push tachometer cable into tachometer housing and secure with screw (**Figure 161**).
24. Install the countershaft sprocket cover (**Figure 162**).
25. Install the shift lever (**Figure 163**).
26. Install carburetors on cylinder heads. Tighten nuts securely (**Figure 164**).
27. Install exhaust pipes and mufflers.

4

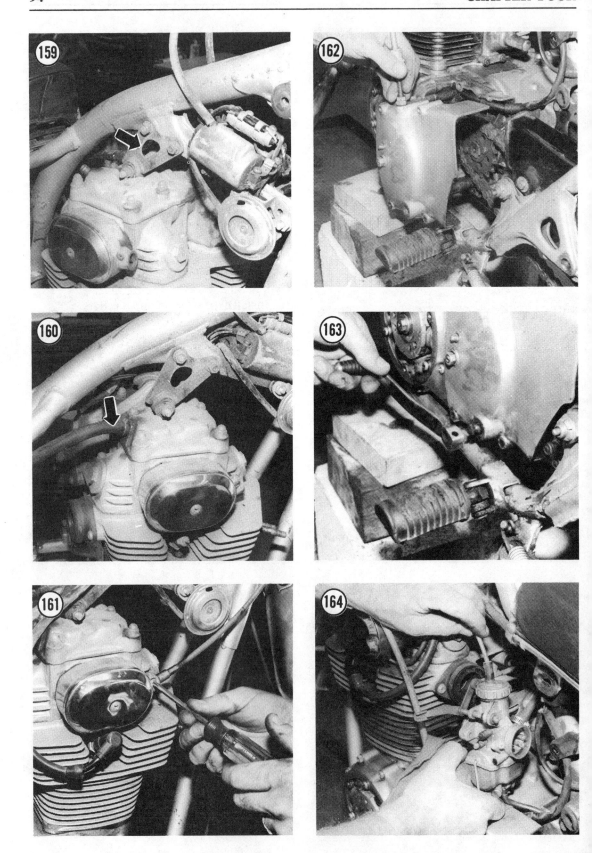

28. Install air filters and secure with 2 bolts (**Figure 165**). Install air filter clamp and tighten screw (**Figure 166**).

Final Checks

1. Fill crankcase with fresh engine oil.
2. Check engine mounting bolts for tightness as a final precaution.

3. Adjust the clutch, throttle cable, drive chain, ignition timing, and valves (refer to Chapter Three for procedures).

4. Inspect all nuts and bolts for tightness.

5. Check wiring for chafing or binding after engine installation.

6. Start engine and check for oil or fuel leaks.

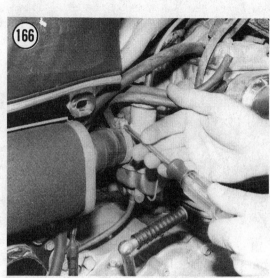

4

CHAPTER FIVE

FUEL AND EXHAUST SYSTEMS

For proper operation, a gasoline engine must be supplied with fuel and air, mixed in proper proportions by weight. A mixture in which there is excess fuel is said to be rich. A lean mixture is one which contains insufficient fuel. It is the function of the carburetor to supply a proper mixture to the engine under all operating conditions.

There are 2 different type carburetors used on the various models covered in this manual. One is the constant velocity or CV type and the other is the slide type. Refer to the correct procedure for your specific model.

CARBURETOR OVERHAUL

There is no set rule regarding frequency of carburetor overhaul. A carburetor used on a machine used primarily for steet riding may go 5,000 miles without attention. If the machine is used in the dirt, the carburetor might need an overhaul in less than 1,000 miles. Poor engine performance, hesitation, and little or no response to idle mixture adjustment are all symptoms of possible carburetor malfunctions.

CARBURETOR (C.V. TYPE)

Removal/Installation

1. Remove the air cleaner covers.

> *NOTE*
> *On models CL250 and CL350, it is necessary to remove the muffler on the left side first.*

2. Remove the clamps, retaining nuts and bolts. Lift off the air cleaner from each side.
3. Remove the carburetor clamps and intake hoses (**Figure 1**).

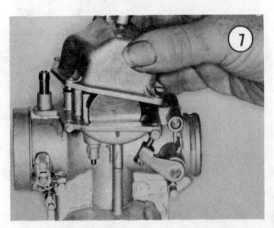

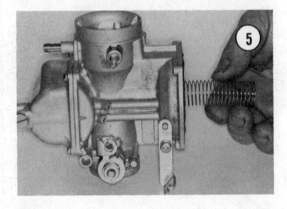

4. Loosen the throttle cables at the throttle twist grip and loosen all routing clamps (**Figure 2**).

5. Pull the carburetor assembly free from the intake tubes. Withdraw it out to one side and disconnect the throttle cables from the assembly.

6. Installation is the reverse of the preceding steps.

Disassembly/Assembly

Refer to **Figure 3** for this procedure.

1. Remove the 4 screws securing the top cover and remove it (**Figure 4**).

2. Pull out the diaphragm return spring (**Figure 5**).

3. Pull out diaphragm/slide assembly (**Figure 6**).

4. Remove the 4 screws securing the float bowl and remove it (**Figure 7**).

5. Remove the 2nd main jet, needle jet, primary main jet, and main jet holder.

6. Remove the float assembly pivot pin (**Figure 8**) and remove the float assembly.

③ CARBURETOR ASSEMBLY (C.V. TYPE)

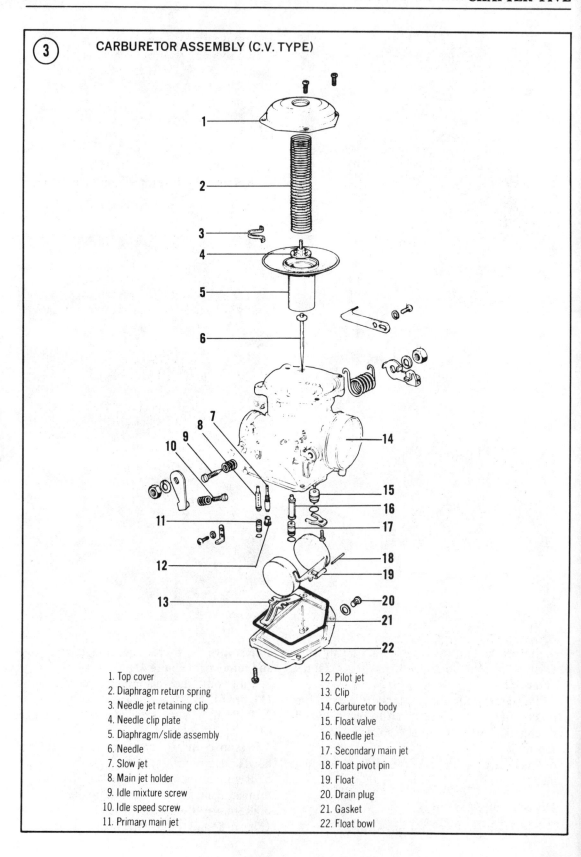

1. Top cover
2. Diaphragm return spring
3. Needle jet retaining clip
4. Needle clip plate
5. Diaphragm/slide assembly
6. Needle
7. Slow jet
8. Main jet holder
9. Idle mixture screw
10. Idle speed screw
11. Primary main jet

12. Pilot jet
13. Clip
14. Carburetor body
15. Float valve
16. Needle jet
17. Secondary main jet
18. Float pivot pin
19. Float
20. Drain plug
21. Gasket
22. Float bowl

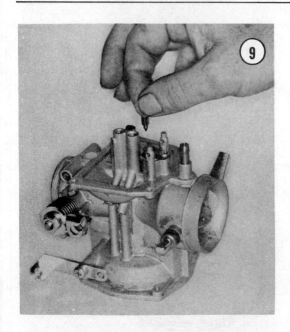

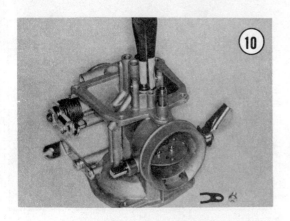

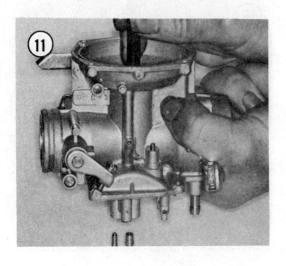

7. Remove the float needle (**Figure 9**).

8. Remove the float valve seat retainer clip. Tape the jaws of a needle nose pliers and pull out the float needle valve seat (**Figure 10**).

9. Push out the pilot jet and slow speed jet. Use a plastic or fiber rod (**Figure 11**). Do not use a metal tool for this operation.

10. Remove the idle mixture screw and spring (**Figure 12**).

11. Remove the float bowl drain plug (**Figure 13**).

12. The needle can be removed from the diaphragm/slide by compressing the jet needle retaining clip with needle nose pliers and removing it.

13. Clean all parts, except rubber or plastic parts, in a good grade of carburetor cleaner. This solution is available at most automotive

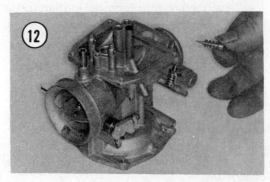

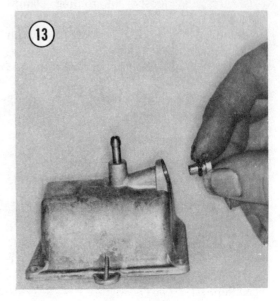

5

or motorcycle supply stores, in a small, resealable tank with a dip basket (**Figure 14**). If it is tightly sealed when not in use, the solution will last for several cleanings. Follow the manufacturer's instructions for correct soak time (usually about 1/2 hour).

NOTE
It is recommended that one carburetor be cleaned at one time to avoid interchanging of parts.

14. Remove the parts from the cleaner and blow dry with compressed air. Blow out the jets with compressed air. DO NOT use a piece of wire to clean them as minor gouges in a jet can alter flow rate and upset the fuel/air mixture.

15. Reverse the preceding steps to assemble the carburetor. Always use new gaskets and O-ring seals upon reassembly. Be sure to check float level before returning the carburetor to service. Refer to *Carburetor Adjustment* following.

CARBURETOR (SLIDE TYPE)

Removal/Installation

1. Remove the side covers. Remove all clamps and retaining nuts and remove the air cleaners from each side.

2. Remove the clamps on each end of the carburetors.

3. Loosen the throttle cables from the throttle twist grip and loosen all routing clamps (**Figure 15**).

4. Remove the carburetor assembly (with cables attached). See **Figure 16**.

5. Disconnect the throttle cables from the assembly.

6. Installation is the reverse of the preceding steps.

Disassembly/Assembly

Refer to **Figure 17** for this procedure.

1. Remove the cap, then pull out the throttle valve and spring (**Figure 18**).

2. Slide off the retaining strap and pull off the float bowl (**Figure 19**).

3. Pull out the float pivot pin, then gently remove the float assembly (**Figure 20**). Take care not to bend the float arm during this operation.

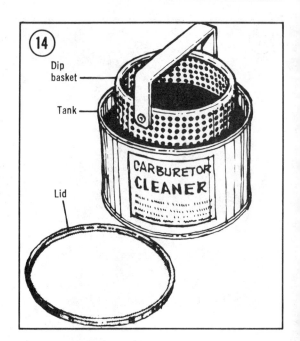

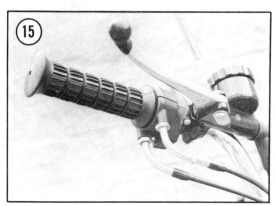

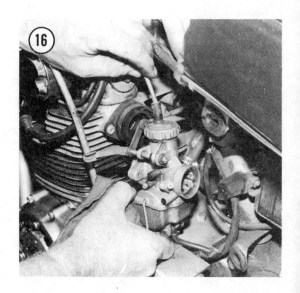

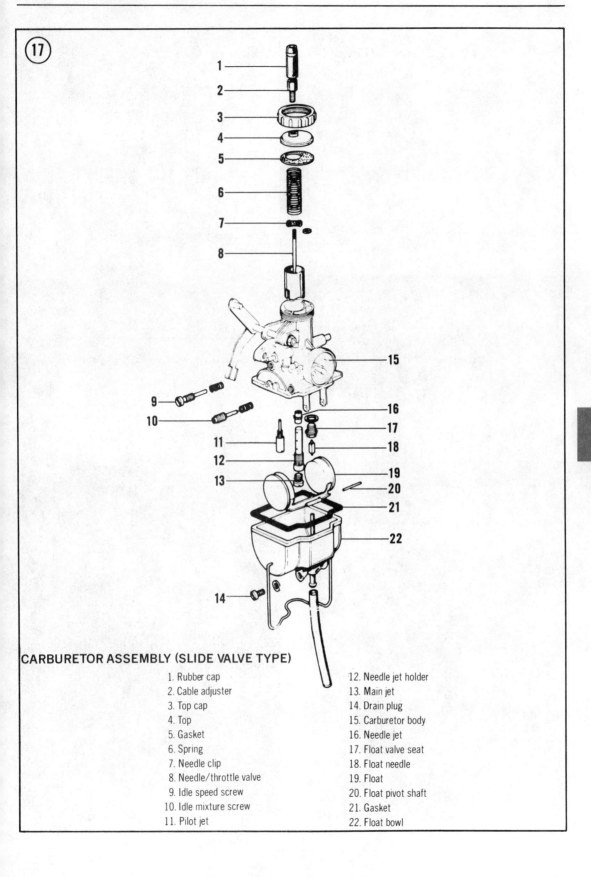

CARBURETOR ASSEMBLY (SLIDE VALVE TYPE)

1. Rubber cap
2. Cable adjuster
3. Top cap
4. Top
5. Gasket
6. Spring
7. Needle clip
8. Needle/throttle valve
9. Idle speed screw
10. Idle mixture screw
11. Pilot jet
12. Needle jet holder
13. Main jet
14. Drain plug
15. Carburetor body
16. Needle jet
17. Float valve seat
18. Float needle
19. Float
20. Float pivot shaft
21. Gasket
22. Float bowl

5

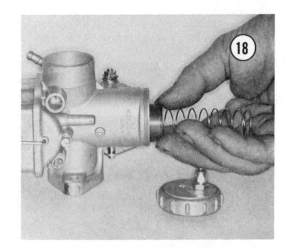

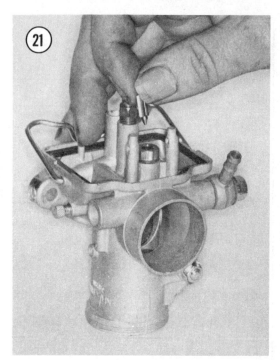

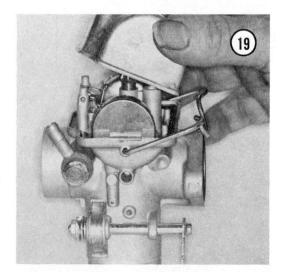

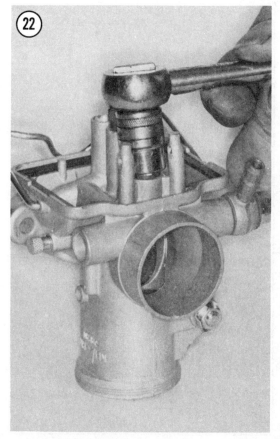

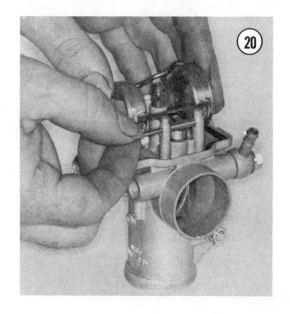

4. Remove the float needle (**Figure 21**).

5. Remove the float valve seat (**Figure 22**). A hooked wire may be used to remove the sealing washer.

6. Remove the needle jet holder and main jet together (**Figure 23**).

7. Push out the needle jet, using a plastic or fiber tool (**Figure 24**). Do not use any metal tool for this operation.

8. Remove the pilot jet (**Figure 25**).

9. Remove the idle speed and idle mixture screws (**Figure 26**). Be careful not to lose either spring.

10. Disassemble the choke mechanism, if necessary, by removing the nut from the end of the choke lever shaft.

11. Remove the O-ring from the mounting flange.

12. Push the jet needle from the throttle slide (**Figure 27**). Do not lose the jet needle retaining clip. Upon reassembly, be sure that the retaining clip does not interfere with the slot in the throttle slide.

13. Separate the main jet from the needle jet holder (**Figure 28**).

14. Remove the drain screw from the float bowl.

15. Remove the banjo fitting (**Figure 29**).

16. Clean all parts, except rubber or plastic parts, in a good grade of carburetor cleaner. This solution is available at most automotive or motorcycle supply stores, in a small, resealable tank with a dip basket (**Figure 14**). If it is tightly sealed when not in use, the solution will last for several cleanings. Follow the manufacturer's instructions for correct soak time (usually about 1/2 hour).

5

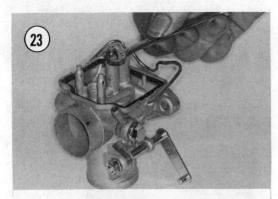

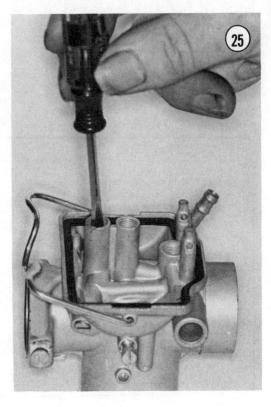

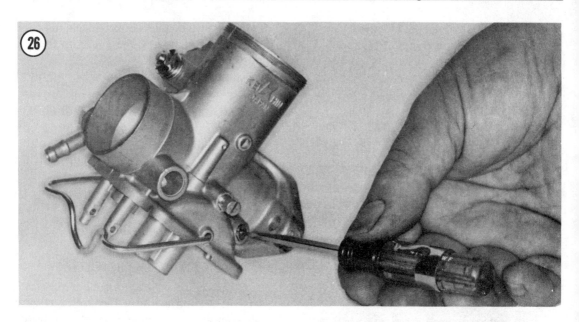

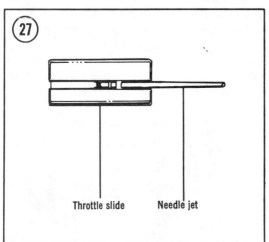

Throttle slide   Needle jet

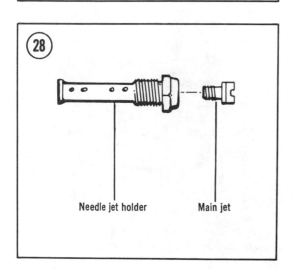

Needle jet holder   Main jet

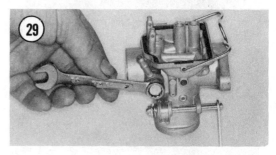

Table 1   CARBURETOR ADJUSTMENT SUMMARY

Throttle Opening	Adjustment	If too Rich	If too Lean
0 - 1/8	Air screw	Turn out	Turn in
1/8 - 1/4	Throttle valve cutaway	Use larger cutaway	Use smaller cutaway
1/4 - 3/4	Jet needle	Raise clip	Lower clip
3/4 - full	Main jet	Use smaller number	Use larger number

BEND TANG TO ADJUST FLOAT LEVEL

Table 2   CARBURETOR FLOAT HEIGHT

Model	Inches	Millimeters
250	0.75	19.0
CB350, CL350		
Prior to engine No. 1045165	0.75	19.0
Engine No. 1045165-1065278	0.83	21.0
Engine No. 1065279-on	1.02	26.0
SL350	0.98	25.0

NOTE
It is recommended that one carburetor be cleaned at one time to avoid interchanging of parts.

17. Remove the parts from the cleaner and blow dry with compressed air. Blow out the jets with compressed air. DO NOT use a piece of wire to clean them as minor gouges in a jet can alter flow rate and upset the fuel/air mixture.

18. Reverse the preceding steps to assemble the carburetor. Always use new gaskets and O-ring seals upon reassembly. Be sure to check float level before returning the carburetor to service. Refer to *Carburetor Adjustment* following.

CARBURETOR ADJUSTMENT

The carburetor is designed to provide the proper mixture under all operating conditions. Little or no benefit will result from experimenting. However, unusual operating conditions such as sustained operation at high altitudes or unusually high or low temperatures may make modifications to standard specifications desirable. The adjustments described in the following paragraphs should only be undertaken if the rider has definite reason to believe they are required. Make the tests and adjustments in the order specified. Float level should be checked each time the carburetor is disassembled, and adjusted if necessary.

A summary of carburetor adjustments is given in **Table 1**.

Float Level (All Types)

To check float level, refer to **Figure 30**.

1. Tilt the carburetor slowly until the tang on the float just barely touches the float needle.

2. Measure the distance between the bottom of the float and the bottom surface of the carburetor body (**Figure 30**). This distance must be as specified in **Table 2**, and equal for both floats. Bend the tang on the float arm (**Figure 31**) as necessary if any adjustment is required.

Jet Size

Make a road test at full throttle for final determination of main jet size. To make such a test, operate the motorcycle at full throttle for at least 2 minutes, then shut the engine off,

5

Table 3   POOR MIXTURE SYMPTOMS

Condition	Symptom
Rich mixture	Rough idle
	Black exhaust smoke
	Hard starting, especially when hot
	Black deposits in exhaust pipes
	Gas-fouled spark plugs
	Poor gas mileage
	Engine performs worse as it warms up
Lean mixture	Backfiring
	Rough idle
	Overheating
	Hesitation upon acceleration
	Engine speed varies at fixed throttle
	Loss of power
	White color on spark plug insulators
	Poor acceleration

release the clutch, and bring the machine to a
stop. If at full throttle the engine runs
"heavily," the main jet is too large. If the
engine runs better by closing the throttle
slightly, the main jet is too small. The engine
will run at full throttle evenly and regularly if
the main jet is of the correct size.

After each such test, remove and examine
the spark plugs. If the insulators have black
sooty deposits, the mixture is too rich. If there
are signs of intense heat, such as a blistered
white appearance, the mixture is too lean.

As a general rule, main jet size should be
reduced approximately 5% for each 3,000 feet
(1,000 meters) above sea level.

Table 3 lists symptoms caused by rich and
lean mixtures.

Idle Speed and Mixture
Adjustment (C.V. Type)

1. Start the engine and allow to warm to
operating temperature.
2. Adjust each idle speed screw so that the
engine idles at 1,000-1,200 rpm (**Figure 32**).
3. Place one hand behind each muffler and
adjust idle speed screw (**Figure 32**) until
exhaust pressure from each muffler is equal.

4. Turn left cylinder idle mixture screw (**Figure 33**) in either direction, slowly, until engine idle speed is at its maximum.

5. Repeat Step 4 for the right cylinder.

6. Check exhaust pressure from each cylinder (as in Step 3) and adjust either idle speed screw necessary to equalize pressures.

7. Turn each idle speed screw an equal amount to obtain 1,000-1,200 rpm idle speed.

8. Synchronize both carburetors (refer to last procedure, this section).

Idle Speed and Mixture Adjustment (Slide Type)

1. Start engine and allow it to warm to operating temperature, then shut it off.

2. Turn each idle mixture screw in until it seats lightly, then back out each one 1-1/4 turns (**Figure 34**).

3. Start the engine. Adjust each idle speed screw so that the engine idles at 1,000-1,200 rpm (**Figure 35**).

4. Place one hand behind each muffler and adjust idle speed screw (refer to **Figure 35**) until exhaust pressure from each muffler is equal.

5. Turn left cylinder idle mixture screw in either direction, slowly, until engine idle speed is at its maximum.

6. Repeat Step 5 for the right cylinder.

7. Check exhaust pressure from each cylinder (as in Step 4) and adjust either idle speed screw if necessary to equalize the pressure.

8. Turn each idle speed screw an equal amount to obtain 1,000-1,200 rpm idle speed.

9. Synchronize both carburetors. See *Synchronizing the Carburetors.*

If the preceding procedure does not work well, due to both carburetors being too far out of adjustment, use the following procedure:

1. Turn the idle mixture screw on each carburetor in until it seats lightly, then back it out 1-1/4 turns (refer to **Figure 34**).

2. Start the engine, then ride the bike long enough to warm it thoroughly.

3. Stop the engine and disconnect either spark plug lead.

4. Restart the engine on one cylinder. Turn the idle speed screw on the "working" cylinder's carburetor in enough to keep the engine running (refer to **Figure 35**).

5. Turn the idle speed screw out until the engine runs slower and begins to falter.

6. Turn the idle mixture screw in or out to make the engine run smoothly. Note the speed indicated on the tachometer.

7. Repeat Steps 5 and 6 to achieve the lowest possible idle speed.

8. Stop the engine, then reconnect the spark plug lead that was disconnected.

9. Repeat Steps 3 through 8 for the other cylinder, matching the engine speed with that observed in Step 6.

10. Start the engine, then turn each idle speed screw an equal amount until the engine idles at 1,000-1,200 rpm.

11. Place one hand behind each muffler and check that the exhaust pressures are equal. If not, turn either idle speed screw in or out until they are.

12. Adjust carburetor synchronization (see following procedure).

Carburetor Synchronization (C.V. Type)

To synchronize the carburetors, proceed as follows:

1. Twist the throttle grip and see if both throttle valves move at the same time.

5

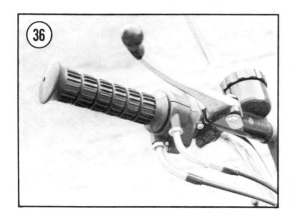

NOTE
Place a hand under the carburetor and note the movement of the throttle levers. They should start to move at the same time.

2. If adjustment is necessary, loosen the throttle cable locknut at the carburetors and adjust the cable adjuster bolt. Tighten the locknut.

Carburetor Synchronization (Slide Type)

To synchronize the carburetors, proceed as follows:
1. Twist the throttle grip and see if both throttle slides begin to move at the same time (**Figure 36**).
2. If throttle slides need adjusting, turn the cable adjuster at the top of either carburetor until the slides move together perfectly (**Figure 37**).

NOTE
A small mirror may be helpful during this check.

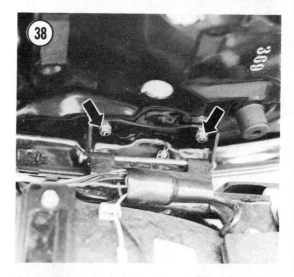

MISCELLANEOUS CARBURETOR PROBLEMS

Water in the carburetor float bowls and sticking carburetor slide valves can result from careless washing of the motorcycle. To remedy this problem, remove and clean the carburetor bowl, main jet, and any other affected parts. Be sure to cover the air intake when washing the machine.

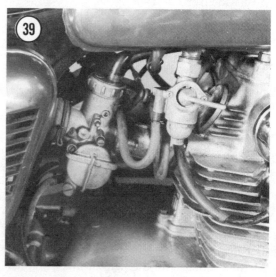

Table 4	CARBURETOR JETS	
Model	Pilot Jet	Main Jet
250	35	68 (primary)
		95 (secondary)
CB350	38	60 (primary)
		115 (secondary)
CL350	38	60 (primary)
		115 (secondary)
SL350	40	120

3. Detach fuel tank from its rear rubber mount; lift it upward and to the rear. Be sure that no wires catch on the tank as it is removed (**Figure 40**).

4. Reverse preceding steps to install the fuel tank.

If gasoline leaks past the float bowl gasket, high speed fuel starvation may occur. Varnish deposits on the outside of the bowl are evidence of this condition.

Dirt in the fuel may lodge in the float valve and cause an overrich mixture. As a temporary measure, tap the carburetor lightly with any convenient small tool to dislodge the dirt. Clean the fuel tank, petcock, fuel line, and carburetor at first opportunity, should this situation occur.

Inspection

1. Be sure that the filler cap vent is not clogged.

2. Check all rubber mounts, and replace them if they are damaged.

3. Check fuel lines for leaks, hardening, or cracks.

4. Check for sediment in the tank, and flush out if necessary.

CARBURETOR SPECIFICATIONS

Table 4 lists major specifications of carburetors of the more popular bikes covered by this manual. These specifications have been determined by exhaustive factory tests, and should not be changed unless there is good reason for doing so.

CAUTION
Open flames, cigarettes, water heater or clothes dryer pilot lights, or electrical sparks may trigger a fatal explosion. Do not work on any fuel system component within 50 feet of any possible source of ignition.

Fuel Strainer Service

The fuel strainer filters out particles which might otherwise get into a carburetor and cause the float needle valve to remain open, resulting in flooding. Such particles might also get into the engine and cause damage.

Remove the fuel strainer, located at the fuel petcock (**Figure 39**), and clean it in solvent, then blow dry with compressed air. Be sure that all gaskets are in good condition upon reassembly.

FUEL TANK

Removal/Installation

1. Loosen seat mounting bolts, then remove the seat (**Figure 38**).

2. Be sure that the fuel flow is shut off at the petcock, then remove fuel lines at petcock (**Figure 39**).

5

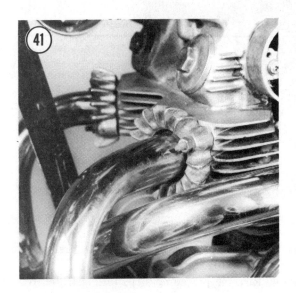

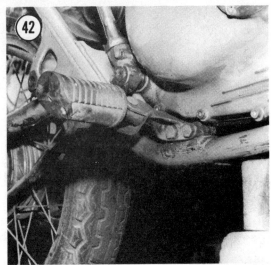

EXHAUST SYSTEM

Removal/Installation

1. Remove nuts at each cylinder head (**Figure 41**).
2. Remove footpegs and footrest bar if necessary (**Figure 42**).
3. Remove rear attachment bolts (**Figure 43**).

NOTE
This attachment point differs with the different models.

4. Reverse preceding steps to install the exhaust system.

Inspection

1. Check gaskets and rubber cushions for cracks or damage.
2. Pull out baffle tubes (if so equipped) and remove carbon deposits.

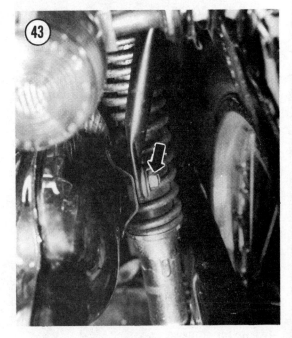

CHAPTER SIX

ELECTRICAL SYSTEM

This chapter covers operating principles and removal and installation procedures for Honda ignition and electrical systems. Refer to Chapter Three for tune-up procedures; refer to Chapter Two for troubleshooting procedures.

IGNITION SYSTEM

Honda twin-cylinder models are equipped with a battery and coil ignition system, similar in many ways to a conventional automobile.

Circuit Operation

Figure 1 illustrates a typical battery ignition system for a single cylinder. When the breaker points are closed, current flows from the battery through the primary windings of the ignition coil, thereby building a magnetic field around the coil. The breaker cam rotates at one-half crankshaft speed and is so adjusted that the breaker points open as the piston reaches firing position.

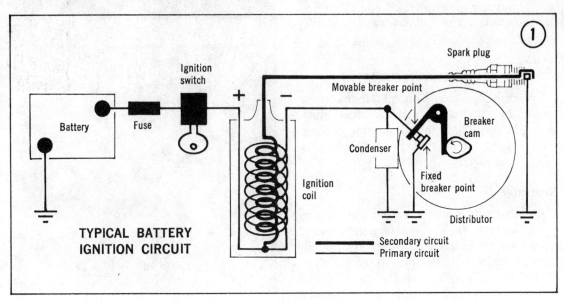

TYPICAL BATTERY IGNITION CIRCUIT

Spark plug · Ignition switch · Movable breaker point · Breaker cam · Battery · Fuse · Condenser · Fixed breaker point · Ignition coil · Distributor · Secondary circuit · Primary circuit

As the points open, the magnetic field collapses. When this happens, a very high voltage is induced (up to approximately 15,000 volts) in the secondary winding of the ignition coil. This high voltage is sufficient to jump the gap at the spark plug.

The condenser assists the coil in developing high voltage, and also protects the points. Inductance of the ignition coil primary winding tends to keep a surge of current flowing through the circuit even after the points have started to open. The condenser stores this surge and thus prevents arcing at the points. This circuit is duplicated for each cylinder.

Troubleshooting

Refer to Chapter Two, for any problems related to the electrical system.

Ignition Coil

The ignition coil is a transformer which develops the high voltage required to jump the spark plug gap. The only maintenance required is that of keeping the electrical connections clean and tight, and occasionally checking to see that the coil is mounted securely (**Figure 2**).

Service

There are two major items requiring service on battery ignition models: breaker point service and ignition timing. Both are vitally important to proper engine operation and reliability. Refer to Chapter Three, *Breaker Points* and *Ignition Timing* sections.

CHARGING SYSTEM

The charging system on all Honda twins covered by this manual consists of an alternator, battery, and interconnecting wiring. Some models are also equipped with a solid state voltage regulator.

Alternator

An alternator is an alternating current electrical generator in which a magnetized field rotor revolves within a set of stationary coils called a stator. As the rotor revolves, alternating current is induced in the stator. Stator current is then rectified and used to operate

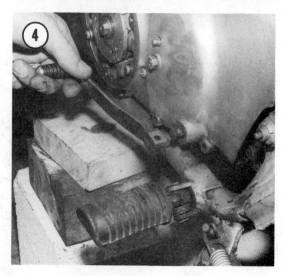

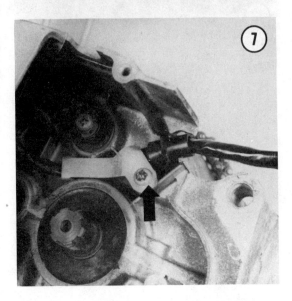

electrical accessories on the motorcycle and for battery charging. Refer to **Figure 3**.

Removal/Installation

1. Remove shift lever (**Figure 4**).

2. Remove alternator cover screws (**Figure 5**) and tap cover off with a rubber mallet (**Figure 6**).

3. Remove clip holding alternator main wiring harness (**Figure 7**).

4. Remove neutral indicator switch (**Figure 8**).

5. Remove alternator retaining nut and pull alternator with a suitable puller (**Figure 9**).

6. Install by reversing the preceding steps.

6

Rectifier

All models are equipped with a full-wave bridge rectifier (**Figure 10**).

> *CAUTION*
> *Always handle the rectifier assembly carefully. Do not bend or try to rotate the wafers. Do not loosen the screws which hold the assembly together. Moisture can damage the assembly, so keep it dry. Never run the engine with the battery disconnected or without a fuse; doing so can cause immediate rectifier destruction.*

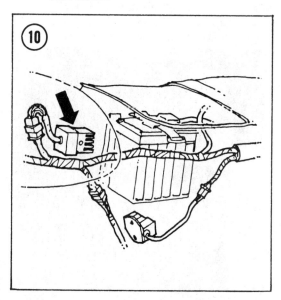

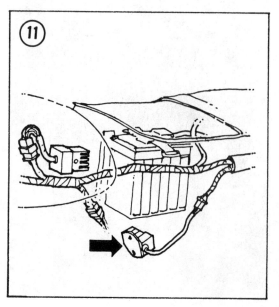

Voltage Regulator

Problems with this unit rarely occur. The voltage regulator is attached to the base of the battery box (**Figure 11**).

> CAUTION
> *Do not connect or disconnect the regulator with the engine running.*

ELECTRIC STARTER

Refer to **Figure 12** for a diagram of a typical starting system.

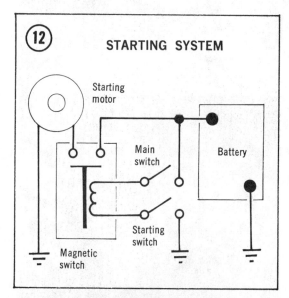

STARTING SYSTEM

Starter Motor

The starter motor (**Figure 13**) is wound in series for high torque, and draws approximately 120 amperes under normal starting conditions. This figure can vary considerably, depending on engine temperature, starter condition, and other factors.

Removal/Installation

1. Remove shift lever (**Figure 14**).

2. Remove alternator cover screws (**Figure 15**) and tap cover off with a rubber mallet (**Figure 16**).

3. Remove starter motor retaining screws (**Figure 17**) and tap starter motor out of case (rearward) with a rubber mallet (**Figure 18**).

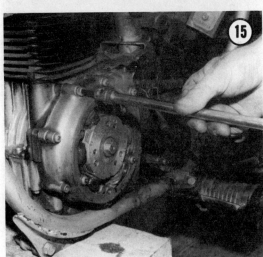

6

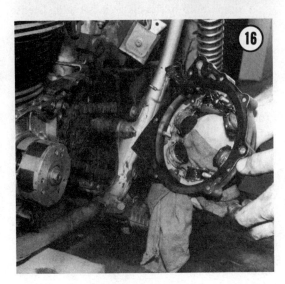

4. Remove chain and sprocket (**Figure 19**).

5. Remove starter sprocket setting plate (**Figure 20**), then remove starter sprocket (if necessary).

6. Install by reversing the preceding steps.

LIGHTS

The headlight assembly consists primarily of a headlight lens and reflector unit, rim, and related hardware.

In the event of lighting problems, first check the affected bulb. Poor ground connections are another cause of lamp malfunctions.

Turn signals usually operate from direct current supplied by the battery. When replacing the signal bulbs, always be sure to use the proper type. Erratic operation or even failure to flash may result from use of wrong bulbs.

Stoplights usually operate from direct current also. Stoplight switches should be adjusted so that the lamp comes on just before braking action begins. Front brake stoplight switches are frequently built into the front brake cable, and are not adjustable.

HEADLIGHT

Replacement

Refer to **Figure 21**.

1. Remove 3 screws and remove headlight from case.

2. Disconnect socket from sealed beam.

3. Remove 2 retaining lock pins and screws from rim.

4. Remove sealed beam.

5. Installation is the reverse of these steps. Adjust headlight as described below.

Adjustment

Adjust headlight horizontally and vertically, according to Department of Motor Vehicle regulations in your state.

To adjust headlight horizontally, turn the screw illustrated in **Figure 22**. To adjust vertically, loosen the bolts on either side of the case. Move the headlight to the desired position, then tighten bolts.

TAIL/STOPLIGHTS

Taillight Replacement

A single bulb performs as a taillight, license plate light, and stoplight. To replace bulb, remove lens and turn bulb counterclockwise.

HORN

Figure 23 is a typical horn circuit. Current for the horn is supplied by the battery. One terminal is connected to the battery through the main switch. The other terminal is grounded when the horn button is pressed.

BATTERY SERVICE

Honda motorcycles are equipped with lead-acid storage batteries, smaller in size but similar in construction, to batteries used in automobiles (**Figure 24**).

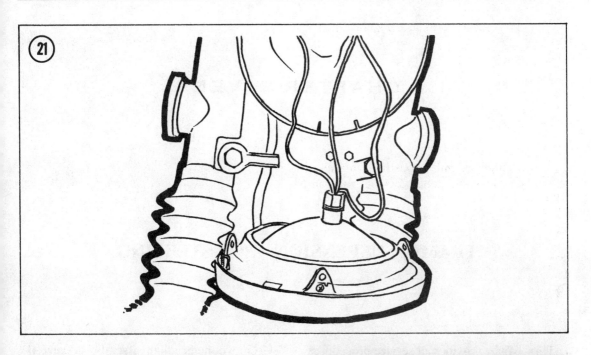

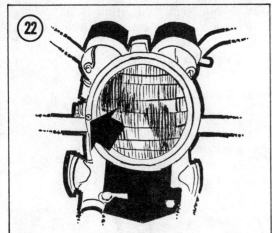

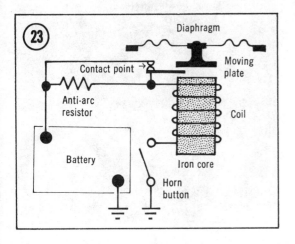

Refer to Chapter Two, *Battery* section, for maintenance procedures.

WIRING DIAGRAMS

Reference to the wiring diagrams at the end of the book will make electrical system troubleshooting easier. Diagrams of all models available are included.

Refer to Chapter Three for troubleshooting procedures.

CHAPTER SEVEN

FRAME, SUSPENSION, AND STEERING

This chapter provides all service procedures for the wheels, brakes, chassis, and related components.

HANDLEBAR

Most manual controls are mounted on the handlebar assembly. Wiring from switches is routed to the headlight, where it is connected to the main wiring harness.

Removal

1. Disconnect the clutch cable at the hand lever (**Figure 1**).
2. On drum brake models, disconnect the brake cable at the hand lever.
3. On disc brake models, remove the 2 bolts (**Figure 2**) securing the master cylinder and lay it on the fuel tank. It is not necessary to remove the hydraulic brake line.

> *CAUTION*
> *Cover the fuel tank with a heavy cloth or plastic tarp to protect it from accidental spilling of brake fluid. Wash any brake fluid off any painted or plated surface immediately, as it will destroy the finish. Use soapy water and rinse thoroughly.*

4. Loosen the clamping screws on the throttle grip assembly and slide it off the handlebar (**Figure 3**).

5. Remove the headlight assembly (**Figure 4**), then disconnect all wiring from the handlebar.
6. Remove bolts and handlebar clamps (**Figure 5**).
7. Lift handlebar from fork top bridge.

Inspection

1. Check cables for chafed or kinked housings. Grease inner cables and be sure that cables operate smoothly.
2. Twist throttle grip. Operation should be smooth throughout its entire travel.

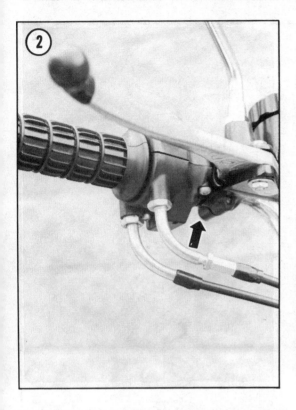

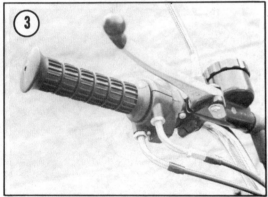

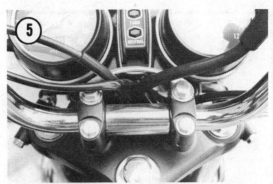

3. Check both hand levers for smooth operation.

4. Check handlebar tubing for cracks or bends.

5. Check switches for proper operation.

6. Inspect wiring for chafed or frayed insulation. Be sure wire terminals are clean and free from corrosion.

Installation

Reverse the *Removal* procedure to install the handlebar. Observe the following notes.

1. Be sure control cables are routed so that they will not be pinched at any position of the front end assembly.

2. Check cables for free movement.

3. Be sure wiring is connected properly.

4. Adjust clutch, front brake, and throttle cables after handlebar service. Refer to Chapter Three for procedures.

FORK TOP BRIDGE

The fork top bridge is mounted on top of the front fork assembly and is retained by the steering stem nut (**Figure 6**).

7

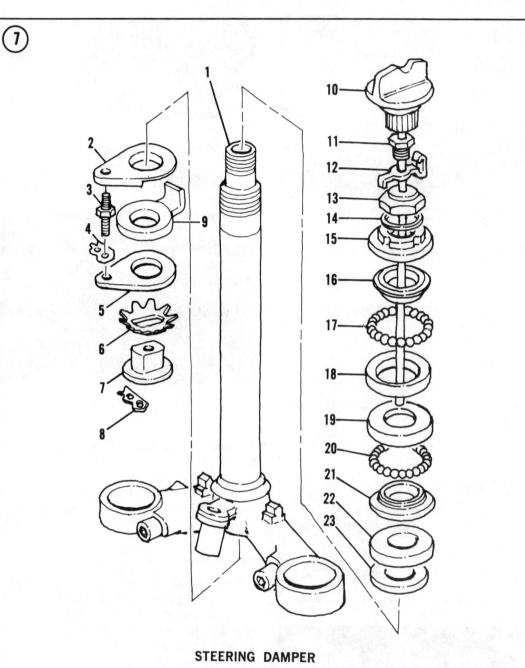

STEERING DAMPER

1. Steering stem
2. Steering damper plate A
3. Friction disc anchor bolt
4. Lock pin
5. Damper plate B
6. Steering damper spring
7. Steering damper nut
8. Lock pin

9. Damper friction disc
10. Steering head top thread
11. Damper lock spring set bolt
12. Damper lock spring
13. Steering stem nut
14. Steering stem washer
15. Steering head top thread
16. Top cone race

17. Steel ball
18. Top race
19. Bottom race
20. Steel ball
21. Bottom cone race
22. Steering head dust seal
23. Dust seal washer

Removal

1. Remove the handlebar assembly (refer to *Handlebar, Removal*, preceding section).
2. Remove steering damper (if so equipped). See **Figure 7**.
3. Disconnect speedometer and tachometer cables (**Figure 8**).
4. Remove front fork top bolts and steering stem nut (**Figure 9**).
5. If so equipped, remove nuts, washers, cushions, and handlebar holders (**Figure 10**).

Inspection

Check for cracks or other damage, and replace worn cushions.

Installation

Reverse the *Removal* procedure, this section, to install the fork top bridge. Observe all notes under *Handlebar, Installation*, Steps 1-4.

STEERING STEM

The steering stem is supported by ball bearings at both ends which enable it to pivot in the frame headpipe (**Figure 11**). Most machines incorporate a steering damper.

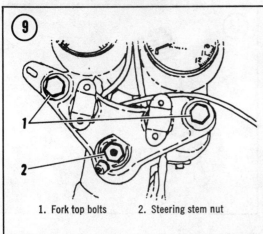

1. Fork top bolts   2. Steering stem nut

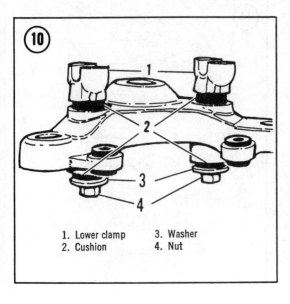

1. Lower clamp   3. Washer
2. Cushion   4. Nut

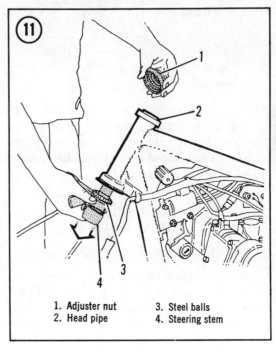

1. Adjuster nut   3. Steel balls
2. Head pipe   4. Steering stem

7

Removal

1. Remove the handlebar (refer to *Handlebar* section this chapter).
2. Remove front wheel (refer to *Wheels* section, this chapter).
3. Remove both front fork legs (refer to *Front Fork* section, this chapter).
4. Remove front fork top bridge (refer to *Fork Top Bridge*, preceding section).
5. Remove steering stem nut (**Figure 12**), then carefully withdraw steering stem downward from frame headpipe (**Figure 13**).

> *NOTE*
> *Be careful not to drop any steel balls.*

Inspection

Examine balls and races for cracks, chips, wear, or other damage. Be sure that dust seals are in good condition. Check for damaged threads. Refer to **Figure 14**.

> *NOTE*
> *Never use any combination of new and used bearings. Replace bearings as complete sets if any defects are found.*

Installation

1. Clean bearings in solvent, then dry and lubricate thoroughly.

> *NOTE*
> *Be careful not to drop any steel balls. Heavy grease will hold them during assembly.*

2. Insert the steering stem upward into the frame headpipe and thread the steering stem nut on. Tighten the nut enough so that the steering stem turns freely without looseness or binding. Refer to **Figure 12**.

FRONT WHEEL (DRUM BRAKE)

Removal/Installation

Refer to **Figure 15** for this procedure.
1. Place a suitable stand under the frame so that the front wheel is off the ground.
2. Unfasten lockwasher and remove hex nut holding the brake stopper arm (**Figure 16**).

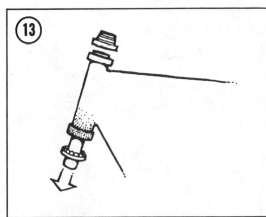

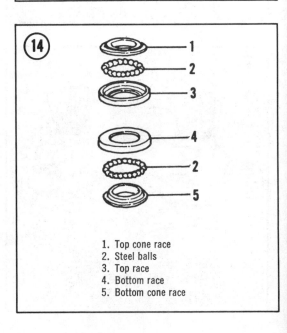

1. Top cone race
2. Steel balls
3. Top race
4. Bottom race
5. Bottom cone race

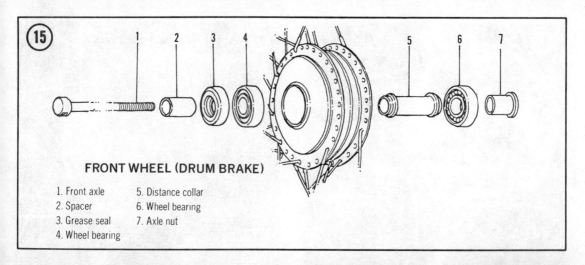

FRONT WHEEL (DRUM BRAKE)

1. Front axle
2. Spacer
3. Grease seal
4. Wheel bearing
5. Distance collar
6. Wheel bearing
7. Axle nut

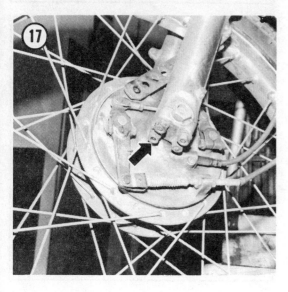

3. Remove fork end cap nuts (**Figure 17**).

4. Remove the speedometer drive screw (**Figure 18**) and pull out the speedometer cable (**Figure 19**).

5. Remove cotter pin and disconnect front brake cable (**Figure 20** and **Figure 21**).

6. Remove fork end cap nuts and fork end cap on other side (**Figure 22**) and remove wheel.

7. Install the wheel by reversing the preceding steps.

8. Adjust the front brake as described in Chapter Three.

Disassembly/Assembly

1. Insert a bar or rod through the hole in the axle end. Remove the axle sleeve with a wrench and remove the axle from the left side.

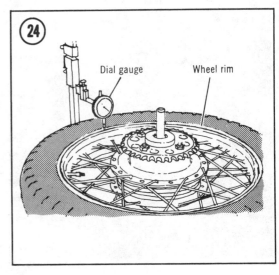

Dial gauge   Wheel rim

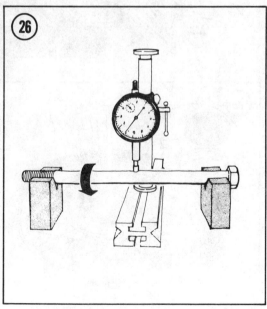

2. Pull the brake assembly straight up and out of the brake drum.

3. Remove the oil seal from the left side.

4. Remove the left and right side bearings and distance collar. Tap the bearings out with a soft aluminum or brass drift.

5. Clean the bearings with solvent and thoroughly dry with compressed air. Do not let the bearings spin while drying. Inspect the bearings for wear and replace if necessary.

6. Pack the bearings with grease. Turn the bearing a couple of times to make sure the grease is distributed evenly inside the bearing.

7. Pack the inside of the hub and distance collar with grease.

8. Install the left and right side bearings and distance collar. Tap the bearings squarely into place and tap on the outer race only. Use a socket (**Figure 23**) that matches the outer race diameter. Do not tap on the inner race or the bearing might be damaged. Be sure that the bearings are completely seated.

9. Install the brake assembly and install the front axle and sleeve.

Inspection

1. Measure the wobble and runout of the wheel rim with a dial indicator as shown in **Figure 24**. The standard value for both wobble and runout is 0.02 in. (0.5mm). The maximum permissible limit is 0.08 in. (2mm).

2. Refer to **Figure 25** and measure the axial and radial runout of the wheel bearing with a dial indicator. Replace the bearing if axial value is more than 0.004 in. (0.1mm) or radial value is more than 0.002 in. (0.05mm).

3. Straighten or replace any bent or loose spokes.

4. Support the axle in V-blocks, or other suitable centering device as shown in **Figure 26**. Rotate the axle through a complete revolution. Straighten or replace the axle if it is bent more than 0.008 in. (0.2mm).

FRONT WHEEL
(DISC BRAKE)

Removal/Installation

Refer to **Figure 27** for this procedure.

7

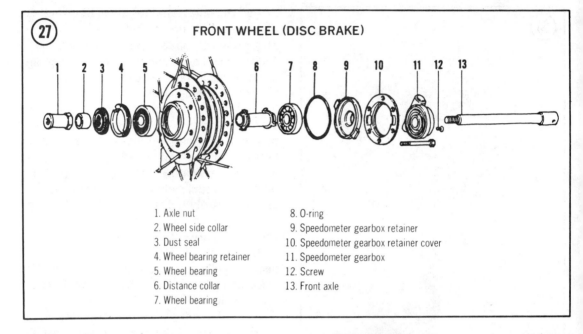

FRONT WHEEL (DISC BRAKE)

1. Axle nut
2. Wheel side collar
3. Dust seal
4. Wheel bearing retainer
5. Wheel bearing
6. Distance collar
7. Wheel bearing
8. O-ring
9. Speedometer gearbox retainer
10. Speedometer gearbox retainer cover
11. Speedometer gearbox
12. Screw
13. Front axle

1. Place a suitable stand under the frame so that the front wheel is off the ground.
2. Remove the screw and disconnect the speedometer cable from the hub (A, **Figure 28**).
3. Loosen the fork end cap nuts (B, **Figure 28**) and end caps and remove the wheel.
4. Install by reversing the preceding steps.

Disassembly/Assembly

1. Remove the bearing retainer from the hub (**Figure 29**). Remove the dust seal from the retainer.
2. Straighten the tangs on the washers (**Figure 30**), then unscrew the mounting bolts securing the disc and remove the disc.
3. Remove the speedometer gearbox and the retainer cover from the other side of the hub.
4. Remove the right and left side wheel bearings and distance collar. Tap the bearings out with a soft aluminum or brass drift.
5. Clean the bearings in solvent and thoroughly dry with compressed air. Do not let the bearing spin while drying. Inspect the bearing for wear and replace as necessary.
6. Pack the bearings with grease. Turn the bearing a couple of times to make sure the grease is distributed evenly inside the bearing.
7. Pack the inside of the hub and distance collar with grease.

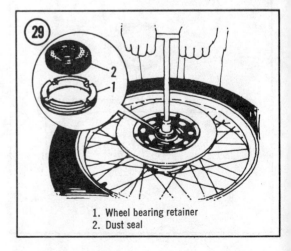

1. Wheel bearing retainer
2. Dust seal

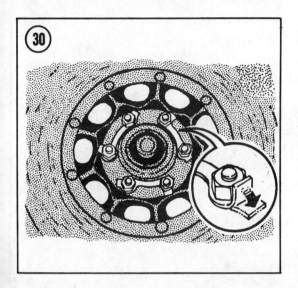

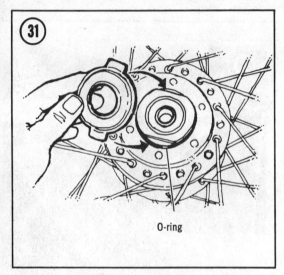

O-ring

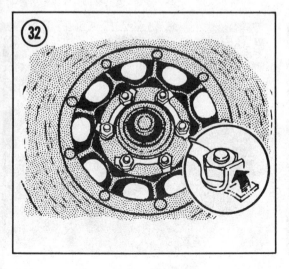

8. Install the left and right side bearing and distance collar. Tap the bearings squarely into place and tap on the outer race only. Use a socket (**Figure 23**) that matches the outer race diameter. Do not tap on the inner race or the bearing might be damaged. Be sure that the bearings are completely seated.

9. Mount the dust seal on the bearing retainer and then install the unit into the hub with the O-ring.

10. Align the speedometer gearbox retainer with the corresponding flat cutouts on the bearing retainer and install as shown in **Figure 31**.

11. Install the brake disc with the mounting bolts and nuts, using new tongued washers. Torque to 15 ft.-lb. (2.0mkg). Then bend the washer tongues, as shown in **Figure 32**, so they will lock the nuts in place.

12. Install the speedometer gear box, then insert the axle through the gearbox into the hub.

13. Install the fork end caps and nuts. Tighten the nuts on the brake disc side first, then tighten the other side.

Inspection

Refer to the preceding *Inspection* procedure for drum brake wheel.

REAR WHEEL

Removal/Installation

Refer to **Figure 33** for this procedure.

1. Remove master link and chain (**Figure 34**).
2. Remove wire safety clip on rear brake torque link (**Figure 35**).
3. Remove nut and washer and remove rear brake torque link (**Figure 36**).
4. On other side, remove cotter pin, axle nut, and washer (**Figure 37**).
5. Remove brake adjusting nut and disconnect brake rod (**Figure 38**).
6. Drive the axle shaft out (**Figure 39**).
7. Pull the wheel to the rear and remove it (**Figure 40**).
8. Insert wheel spacer (**Figure 41**).
9. On the other side, align axle and axle hole. Insert spacer and slide axle shaft in (grease it first). See **Figure 42**.
10. Lightly tighten the axle nut (**Figure 43**).

7

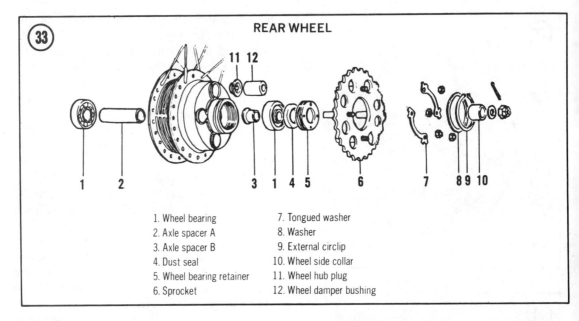

REAR WHEEL

1. Wheel bearing
2. Axle spacer A
3. Axle spacer B
4. Dust seal
5. Wheel bearing retainer
6. Sprocket
7. Tongued washer
8. Washer
9. External circlip
10. Wheel side collar
11. Wheel hub plug
12. Wheel damper bushing

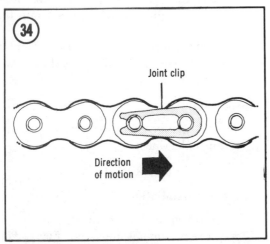

Joint clip

Direction of motion

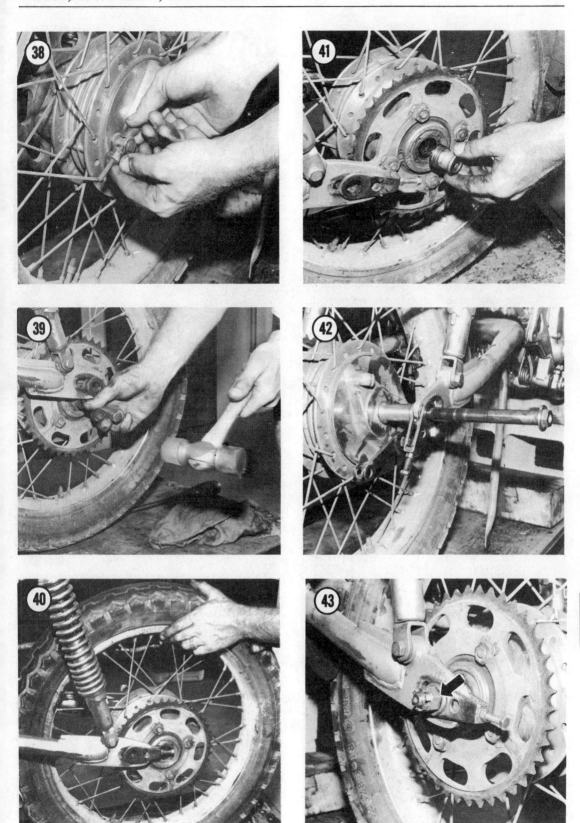

11. Connect rear brake torque link with a washer and nut and install new cotter pin (**Figure 44**).

12. Install chain. Be sure master link is installed exactly as shown in **Figure 34**.

13. Refer to **Figure 45** and connect brake rod and thread brake adjusting nut onto rod. Turn each adjustment bolt (one on each side of wheel) until there is 3/4 to 1 in. (20-25mm) of up-and-down movement in the center of the lower chain run (**Figure 46**). Tighten the adjustment bolt locknuts (one on each side of the wheel).

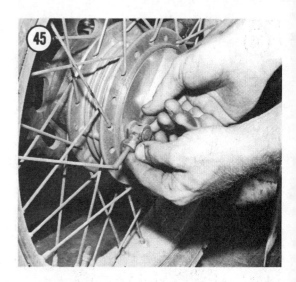

NOTE
*Be sure that the reference marks on the swing arm and the index marks on the chain adjusters are in the same relative positions on each side (**Figure 46**).*

14. Tighten the rear axle nut and install a new cotter pin (**Figure 47**).

15. Adjust the rear brake as described in Chapter Three.

Sprocket Removal/Installation

Remove the sprocket by straightening the tongues on the washers, and unscrewing the 4 mounting bolts (**Figure 48**). Tap the sprocket free with a wood block (**Figure 49**).

Check the teeth on the sprocket (**Figure 50**) for excessive wear; replace if necessary.

Install by reversing the preceding steps.

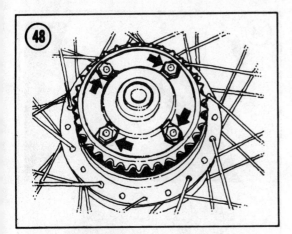

48

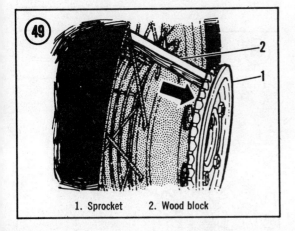

49

1. Sprocket   2. Wood block

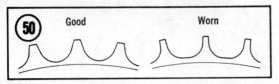

50

Good   Worn

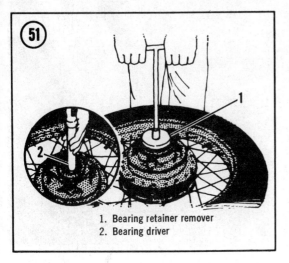

51

1. Bearing retainer remover
2. Bearing driver

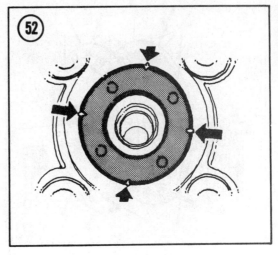

52

Bearing Removal/Installation

1. Remove wheel and sprocket.

2. Drill out stake marks with a 0.25 in. (6mm) drill bit.

3. Remove the bearing retainer (**Figure 51**) and drive the bearings and spacers out of the hub. The retainer has a left-hand thread.

4. Install by reversing the preceding steps. Use Loctite Lock 'N' Seal on the bearing retainer. Stake the bearing retainer with a punch as shown in **Figure 52** in an area apart from the original stake mark locations.

WHEELS (ALL)

Balance

An unbalanced wheel results in unsafe riding conditions. Depending on the degree of unbalance and the speed of the motorcycle, the rider may experience anything from a mild vibration to a violent shimmy which may even result in loss of control. Balance weights are applied on the light side of the wheel to correct this condition.

Before you attempt to balance the wheel, check to be sure that the wheel bearings are in good condition and properly lubricated, that the brakes do not drag, so the wheel rotates freely, and that the rim is true.

1. Mount the wheel on a fixture such as the one in **Figure 53** so it can rotate freely.

2. Give the wheel a spin and let it coast to a stop. Mark the tire at the lowest point.

7

3. Spin the wheel several more times. If the wheel keeps coming to rest at the same point, it is out of balance.

4. Attach a weight to the upper—or light—side of the wheel at the spoke (**Figure 54**). Weights come in 4 sizes: 5, 10, 15, and 20 grams.

5. Experiment with different weights until the wheel, when spun, comes to rest at a different position each time.

Spokes

Spokes should be checked for tightness. The "tuning fork" method of checking spoke tightness is simple and works well. Tap each spoke with a spoke wrench or shank of a screwdriver and listen to the tone. A tightened spoke will emit a clear, ringing tone, and a loose spoke will sound flat. All spokes in a correctly tightened wheel will emit tones of similar pitch but not necessarily the same precise tone.

Bent or stripped spokes should be replaced as soon as they are detected. Unscrew the nipple from the spoke and depress the nipple into the rim far enough to free the end of the spoke, taking care not to push the spoke all the way in. Remove the damaged spoke from the hub and use it to match a new spoke of identical length. If necessary, trim the new spoke to match the original and dress the end of the threads with a die. Install the new spoke in the hub and screw on the nipple, tightening

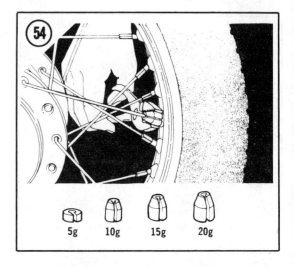

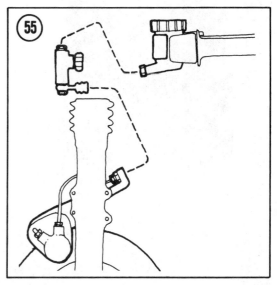

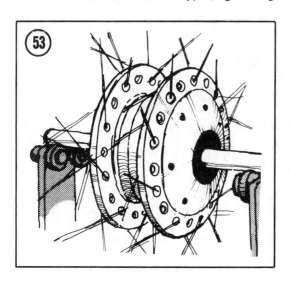

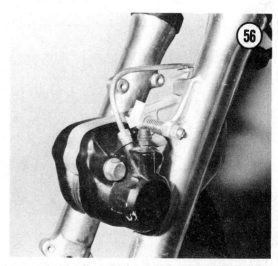

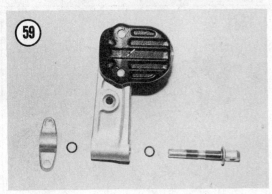

it until the spoke's tone is similar to the tone of the other spokes on the wheel. Periodically check the new spoke; it will stretch and must be retightened several times before it takes a final set.

FRONT DISC BRAKE

The major components of the front disc brake system are shown in **Figure 55**.

Disc Brake Caliper Removal

1. Remove the front wheel as described in this chapter.
2. Disconnect the hydraulic brake line from brake caliper (**Figure 56**). Tie the end of the brake hose up to the handlebar to minimize brake fluid loss.
3. Remove brake caliper retaining bolts and remove the caliper (**Figure 57**).

Disc Brake Caliper Disassembly/Inspection/Assembly

Refer to **Figure 58** for this procedure.
1. Disassemble the caliper to the stage shown in **Figure 59**.
2. Remove bolts shown in **Figure 60** (secure caliper holder in a vise).

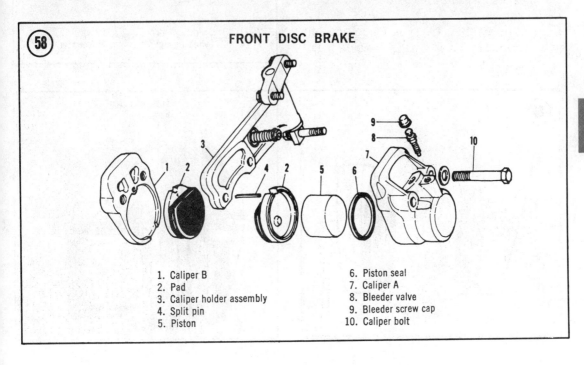

FRONT DISC BRAKE

1. Caliper B
2. Pad
3. Caliper holder assembly
4. Split pin
5. Piston
6. Piston seal
7. Caliper A
8. Bleeder valve
9. Bleeder screw cap
10. Caliper bolt

7

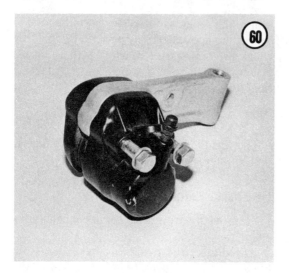

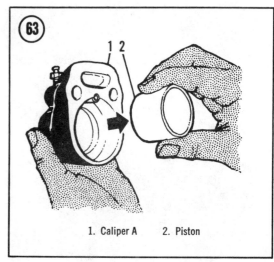

1. Caliper A   2. Piston

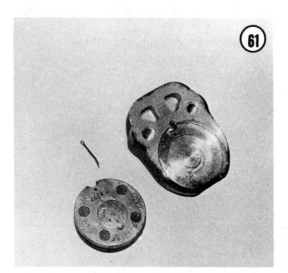

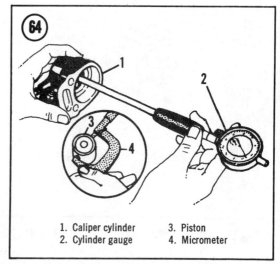

1. Caliper cylinder   3. Piston
2. Cylinder gauge   4. Micrometer

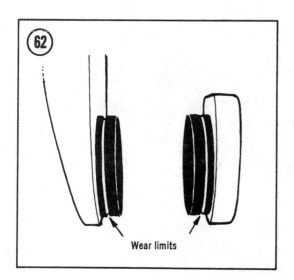

Wear limits

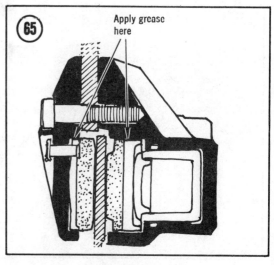

Apply grease here

3. Remove pin on back of the fixed brake pad and remove the pad (**Figure 61**) from caliper "A."

4. Remove the pad from the caliper "B." Inspect both pads for wear; if worn to the red limit line (**Figure 62**) they must be replaced. Always replace as a set.

5. Remove the piston from caliper "A" (**Figure 63**).

6. Measure the inside diameter of the caliper cylinder with a dial indicator and the outer diameter of the piston with a micrometer (**Figure 64**). Compute the clearance by subtraction. If the difference is greater than 0.0043 in. (0.11mm), the parts should be replaced.

7. Check the caliper piston seal for damage; replace if necessary.

8. Assemble by reversing these disassembly steps. Apply a small amount of silicone grease to the calipers as shown in **Figure 65**.

> *WARNING*
> *Do not get grease on the braking surfaces of the pads or brakes will not work. Pads cannot be cleaned; if contaminated, they must be replaced.*

Disc Brake Caliper Installation

1. Install the brake caliper retaining bolts (**Figure 57**).

2. Connect the hydraulic brake line to the caliper (**Figure 56**).

3. Install the front wheel as described in this chapter.

4. Refill the master cylinder with brake fluid and bleed the system (refer to *Bleeding the System* in the following section).

5. After new brake pads are installed, the caliper must be adjusted for correct clearance (this is a one time adjustment). Thereafter the correct clearance will automatically be maintained. The correct clearance between the brake disc and the pad is 0.006 in. (0.15mm). Turn the caliper adjusting bolt counterclockwise until the pad bears up against the disc. Then turn the bolt clockwise 1/2 turn and tighten the locknut. This will give the approximate clearance required.

Master Cylinder Removal/Installation

1. Remove bolt securing the brake hose to the master cylinder.

2. Remove the 2 bolts securing the master cylinder to the handlebar and remove the assembly.

3. Installation is the reverse of these steps.

4. Bleed the system (refer to *Bleeding the System* in the following section).

Master Cylinder Disassembly/Assembly

Refer to **Figure 66** for this procedure.

1. Remove the master cylinder as previously described.

2. Remove the cap, plate, and diaphragm.

3. Remove the stopper washer and boot.

4. Remove the snap ring (**Figure 67**) with snap ring pliers.

5. Remove the washer, piston, secondary and primary cup, spring, and check valve.

6. Clean all parts thoroughly in denatured alcohol or clean brake fluid.

7. Measure cylinder bore with a cylinder gauge (**Figure 68**) and the outer diameter of the piston with a micrometer. Compute the clearance by subtraction. If the difference is greater than 0.0043 in. (0.11mm), the parts should be replaced.

8. Replace primary and secondary cups with new ones.

9. Coat the inside of the master cylinder with fresh brake fluid.

10. Install the check valve and spring as shown in **Figure 69**.

11. Coat the primary cup with fresh brake fluid and install as shown in **Figure 70**.

12. Install the secondary cup, piston, washer, and circlip.

13. Install the boot and stopper washer.

14. Install the diaphragm, plate, and cap.

15. Install on handlebar, refill with fresh brake fluid, and bleed the system.

Bleeding the System

The brake system must be bled any time air enters the system. Air may enter when the bleeder valve is open, because of a leaking hose fitting, or if the reservoir fluid level becomes too low.

7

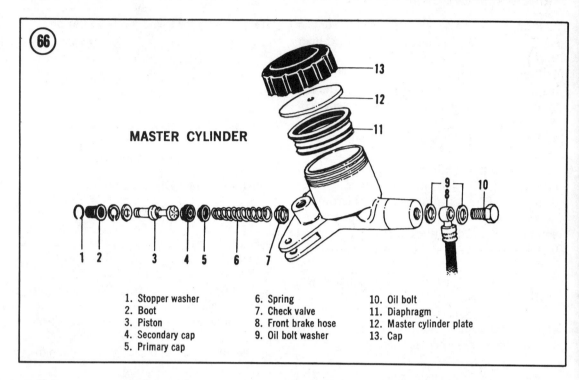

MASTER CYLINDER

1. Stopper washer
2. Boot
3. Piston
4. Secondary cap
5. Primary cap
6. Spring
7. Check valve
8. Front brake hose
9. Oil bolt washer
10. Oil bolt
11. Diaphragm
12. Master cylinder plate
13. Cap

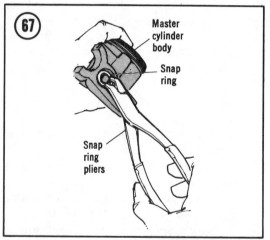

Master cylinder body

Snap ring

Snap ring pliers

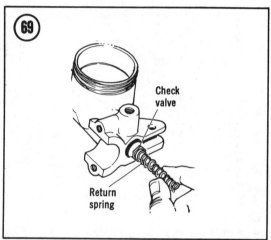

Check valve

Return spring

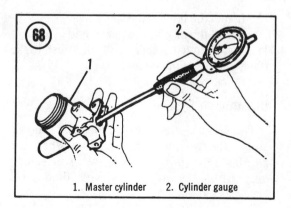

1. Master cylinder   2. Cylinder gauge

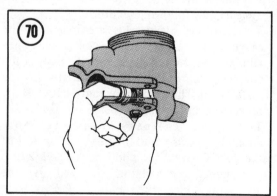

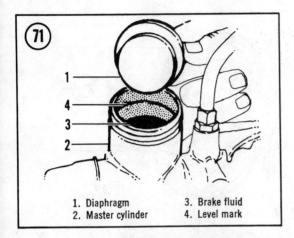

1. Diaphragm   3. Brake fluid
2. Master cylinder   4. Level mark

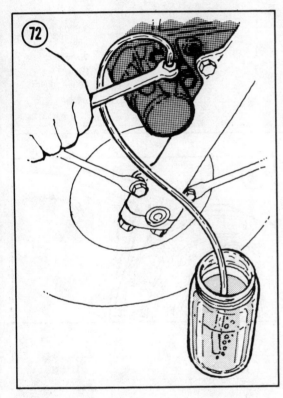

1. Fill the master cylinder brake reservoir with fresh brake fluid (**Figure 71**) to the level mark. Check the level frequently during the bleeding procedure, as some fluid will be lost.

CAUTION
Cover the fuel tank and instrument cluster with a heavy cloth or plastic tarp to protect it from the accidental spilling of brake fluid. Wash any brake fluid off of any

painted or plated surfaces immediately, as it will destroy the finish. Use soapy water and rinse thoroughly.

WARNING
Use brake fluid clearly marked DOT 3 only. Others may vaporize and cause brake failure. Always use the same brand name; do not intermix as many brands are not compatible.

2. Remove the rubber cap from the bleeder valve, then connect a length of clear plastic tubing to the bleeder valve (**Figure 72**). Place the other end of the tube into a clean jar containing fresh brake fluid. Be sure that the end of the tubing remains submerged in brake fluid during the entire operation. If not, air will reenter the system.
3. Open the bleeder valve, squeeze the brake lever slowly, close the valve, and release the lever. Repeat this sequence several times until the tube is full of brake fluid.
4. Open the bleeder valve. With the bleeder valve open, continue to slowly squeeze and release the lever until no bubbles appear in either the brake fluid reservoir or in the fluid flowing from the bleeder valve. Add brake fluid to the reservoir as necessary to maintain the proper level.
5. Close the bleeder valve, install the rubber cap and fill the master cylinder reservoir to the line (**Figure 71**).

DRUM BRAKE (FRONT AND REAR)

Removal/Inspection/Installation

Refer to **Figure 73** for basic brake components.
1. Remove the front or rear wheel as described in this chapter.
2. Pull the brake assembly straight up and out of the drum (**Figure 74**).
3. Measure the inside diameter of the brake drum with vernier calipers (**Figure 75**). Replace if the brake drum is worn beyond the following service limits:

Front drum: 7.17 in. (182mm)
Rear drum: 6.38 in. (162mm)

7

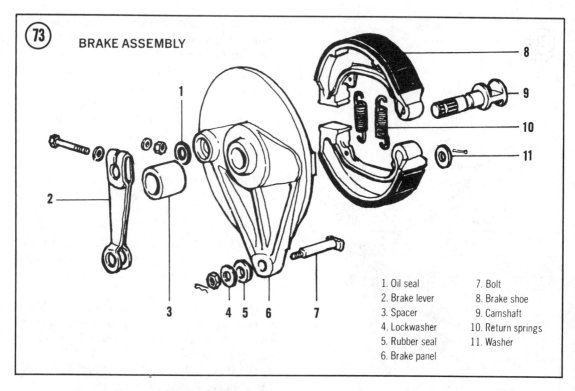

⑬ BRAKE ASSEMBLY

1. Oil seal
2. Brake lever
3. Spacer
4. Lockwasher
5. Rubber seal
6. Brake panel
7. Bolt
8. Brake shoe
9. Camshaft
10. Return springs
11. Washer

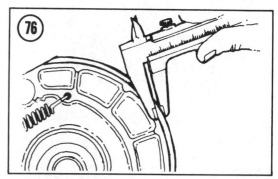

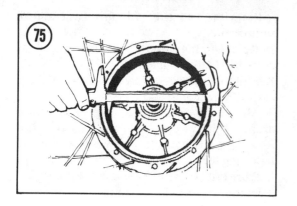

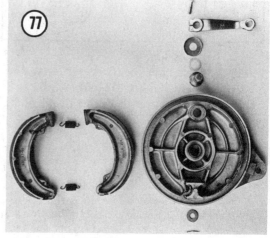

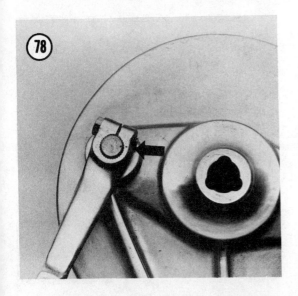

4. Measure the brake lining thickness with vernier calipers (**Figure 76**). Replace if worn to 0.12 in. (3.0mm) of the metal shoe table.

5. To replace the brake shoes refer to **Figure 77** (this is the rear brake assembly but the front is almost identical). Remove the cotter pin, washer, spring, and brake shoes. Reverse disassembly procedure to reassemble the brake assembly.

NOTE
*If brake arms have been removed, be sure that the punch mark on the brake arm aligns with the corresponding mark on the brake cam (**Figure 78**).*

6. **Figure 79** shows the brake assembly completely assembled.

FRONT SUSPENSION

The front suspension consists of a front fork assembly that serves as a shock absorber for the front wheel. There are 4 different configurations of forks used on the various models covered in this manual. They are as follows:

   a. Piston type
   b. Rod type
   c. Piston valve type (SL350 only)
   d. Free valve type (SL350 only)

The removal and installation of the fork assemblies from the bike's frame are basically the same for all models and are covered only once at the beginning of this section. Disassembly, inspection, and assembly all vary and are covered separately.

Removal/Installation

1. Place a pan under the fork assembly, then remove the drain screw at the lower end of each fork leg (**Figure 80**). Allow the oil to drain for about 10-15 minutes. With the front brake applied, pump the forks several times to force oil out.

CAUTION
Do not allow the fork oil to come in contact with any of the brake components.

2. Remove the front wheel as described in this chapter.

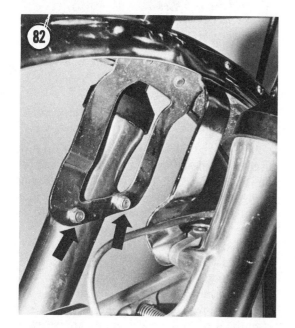

Table 1   FORK OIL CAPACITY (AFTER DISASSEMBLY)

Model	Ounces	Cubic Centimeters
CB & CL250,350	6.6-6.9	195-205
CB & CL250, 350K1,K2,K3 CB250, 350K4, CL350K4, CB350G, CL350K5	4.2-4.4	125-130
SL350, SL350K1, SL350K2	6.1-6.4	180-190

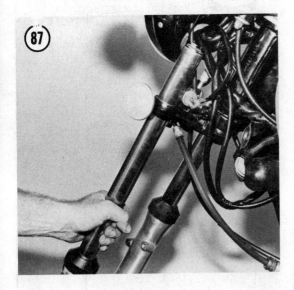

3. Remove the headlight assembly (**Figure 81**).

4. Remove the fender bolts (**Figure 82**).

5. On models with disc brakes, remove the caliper assembly (**Figure 83**). Tie the caliper assembly up to the handlebar to remove any strain on the hydraulic brake line.

6. On models with disc brakes, remove the Honda nameplate (**Figure 84**).

7. Loosen the top crown pinch bolts (**Figure 85**).

8. Loosen the bottom crown pinch bolts (**Figure 86**).

9. With a twisting motion, pull the forks down and out (**Figure 87**).

10. Installation is the reverse of the removal steps, noting the following.

11. Fill each fork leg with fresh fork oil; refer to **Table 1** for the correct type and quantity.

FRONT FORK (PISTON TYPE)

Disassembly/Inspection/Assembly

Refer to **Figure 88** for this procedure.

1. Remove the fork cap bolt (16) and remove the fork boot (24).

2. On models CB250 and CB350 remove the fork under cover.

3. Remove the spring (11) and spring seat (26).

4. Remove the internal 44mm circlip (14) with circlip pliers (**Figure 89**).

5. Pull out the fork tube (13) from the slider (9).

6. Remove in the following order the snap ring, fork piston, piston stopper ring, damper valve, valve stopper ring, fork pipe stopper ring, and fork tube guide (**Figure 90**).

7. Clean all parts in solvent and thoroughly dry.

8. Check the fork tube for signs of wear or galling.

9. Check the lower slider for dents or exterior damage that may cause the upper fork tube to hang up during riding conditions.

10. Measure the uncompressed free length of the cushion spring with vernier calipers. Replace the spring if the dimension is 7.72 in. (196mm) or less.

11. Measure the outside diameter of the fork piston with a micrometer (**Figure 91**). Replace if the dimension is 1.472 in. (37.385mm) or less.

12. Measure the inside diameter of the lower slider with a cylinder gauge (**Figure 92**). If the dimension is 1.484 in. (37.680mm) or greater it must be replaced.

7

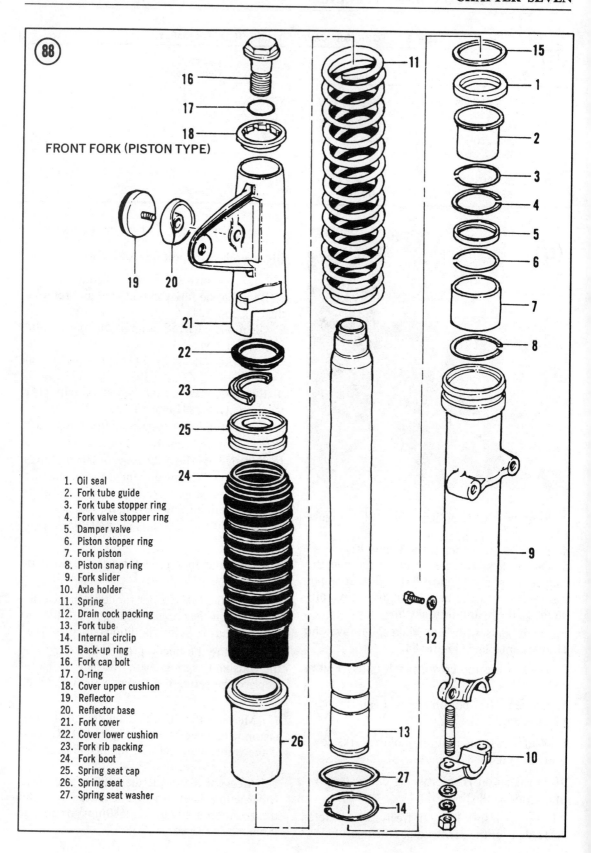

88

FRONT FORK (PISTON TYPE)

16
17
18
19 20
21
22
23
25
24

11
15
1
2
3
4
5
6
7
8
9
13
12
27
14
10

1. Oil seal
2. Fork tube guide
3. Fork tube stopper ring
4. Fork valve stopper ring
5. Damper valve
6. Piston stopper ring
7. Fork piston
8. Piston snap ring
9. Fork slider
10. Axle holder
11. Spring
12. Drain cock packing
13. Fork tube
14. Internal circlip
15. Back-up ring
16. Fork cap bolt
17. O-ring
18. Cover upper cushion
19. Reflector
20. Reflector base
21. Fork cover
22. Cover lower cushion
23. Fork rib packing
24. Fork boot
25. Spring seat cap
26. Spring seat
27. Spring seat washer

26

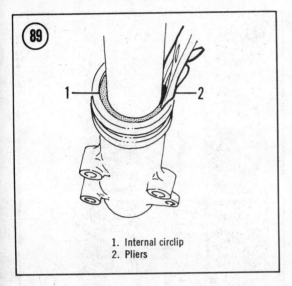

89

1. Internal circlip
2. Pliers

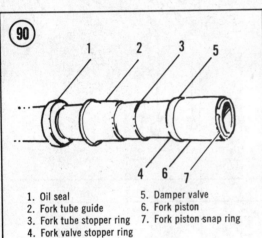

90

1. Oil seal
2. Fork tube guide
3. Fork tube stopper ring
4. Fork valve stopper ring
5. Damper valve
6. Fork piston
7. Fork piston snap ring

91

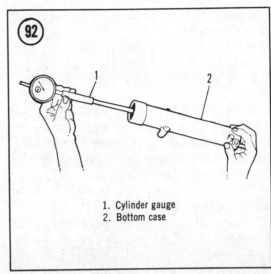

92

1. Cylinder gauge
2. Bottom case

13. Clean all parts again in solvent and thoroughly dry. Coat the new oil seal (1) with fresh fork oil.

14. Assemble the fork tube guide, fork pipe stopper ring, valve stopper ring, damper valve, piston stopper ring, fork piston and the snap ring (**Figure 90**).

15. Install the fork tube assembly into the fork slider and install the oil seal with special tools (**Figure 93**). Take care not to damage the oil seal during installation.

NOTE
These special tools can be improvised. Start the oil seal in by hand, then lay a large washer over it. Drive the seal in with a piece of pipe, which can slide over the fork tube. Make sure the pipe does not mar the fork tube during this procedure. Wrap the fork tube with duct tape to protect it. Make sure the seal is completely seated.

16. Install the internal circlip (**Figure 89**).

FRONT FORK (ROD TYPE)

Disassembly/Inspection/Assembly

Refer to **Figure 94** for this procedure.
1. Remove the fork cap bolt (12).
2. Remove the locknut (11).
3. Remove the spring (9) and spring seat (8).
4. Place the slider in a vise with soft jaws and remove the 8mm bolt (3) securing the damper (5).

7

5. Remove the internal circlip (7) with circlip pliers (**Figure 95**).

6. Pull the fork tube out of the slider and remove the oil seal (6) from the slider.

7. Clean all parts in solvent and thoroughly dry.

8. Check the fork tube for signs of wear or galling.

9. Check the lower slider for dents or exterior damage that may cause the upper fork tube to hang up during riding conditions.

10. Inspect the fork spring for wear or distortion, replace if necessary.

11. Clean all parts again in solvent and thoroughly dry. Coat the new oil seal with fresh fork oil.

12. Install the fork tube assembly into the fork slider and install the oil seal with special tools (**Figure 93**). Take care not to damage the oil seal during installation.

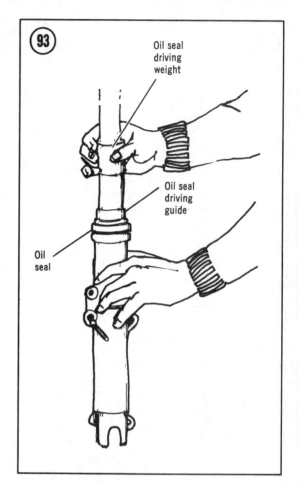

NOTE

These special tools can be improvised. Start the oil seal in by hand, then lay a large washer over it. Drive the seal in with a piece of pipe, which can slide over the fork tube. Make sure the pipe does not mar the fork tube during this procedure. Wrap the fork tube with duct tape to protect it. Make sure the seal is completely seated.

13. Install the internal circlip (**Figure 95**).

14. Apply Loctite Lock'N'Seal to the threads of the 8mm bolt and install it. Tighten it securely.

15. Install the spring seat (8) and spring (9).

16. Apply Loctite Lock'N'Seal to the threads on the damper (5) and install the locknut (11). Tighten it securely.

17. Temporarily install the cap bolt until the fork is reinstalled and refilled with fork oil.

FRONT FORK
(PISTON VALVE TYPE)

Disassembly/Inspection/Assembly

Refer to **Figure 96** for this procedure.

1. Remove the fork cap bolt (1).

2. Remove the fork dust seal (3).

3. Remove the internal 48mm circlip (5) with circlip pliers (**Figure 95**).

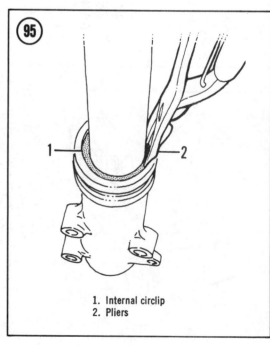

1. Internal circlip
2. Pliers

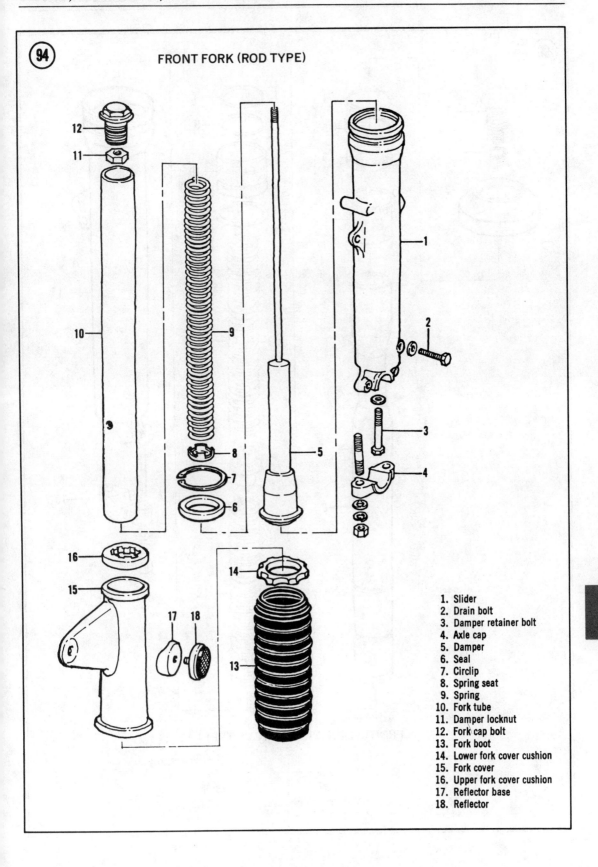

FRONT FORK (ROD TYPE)

1. Slider
2. Drain bolt
3. Damper retainer bolt
4. Axle cap
5. Damper
6. Seal
7. Circlip
8. Spring seat
9. Spring
10. Fork tube
11. Damper locknut
12. Fork cap bolt
13. Fork boot
14. Lower fork cover cushion
15. Fork cover
16. Upper fork cover cushion
17. Reflector base
18. Reflector

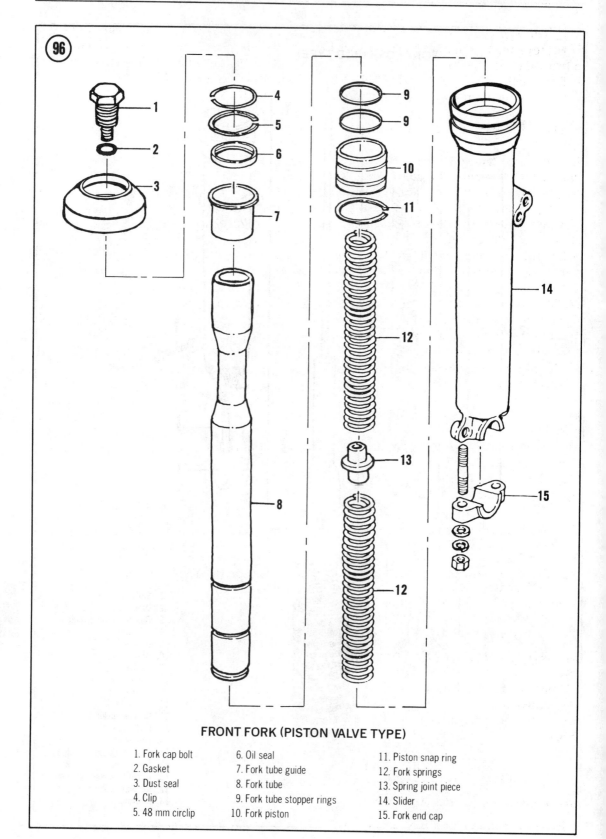

FRONT FORK (PISTON VALVE TYPE)

1. Fork cap bolt
2. Gasket
3. Dust seal
4. Clip
5. 48 mm circlip
6. Oil seal
7. Fork tube guide
8. Fork tube
9. Fork tube stopper rings
10. Fork piston
11. Piston snap ring
12. Fork springs
13. Spring joint piece
14. Slider
15. Fork end cap

4. Pull the fork tube (8) out of the slider (14).

5. Remove the 2 springs (12) and the spring joint piece (13).

6. Remove the oil seal (6) from the slider.

7. Clean all parts in solvent and thoroughly dry.

8. Check the fork tube for signs of wear or galling.

9. Check the lower slider for dents or exterior damage that may cause the upper fork tube to hang up during riding conditions.

10. Inspect the condition of the fork springs for wear or distortion; replace as necessary.

11. Measure the outside diameter of the fork piston with a micrometer (**Figure 91**). Replace if the dimension is 1.472 in. (37.385mm) or less.

12. Measure the inside diameter of the lower slider with a cylinder gauge (**Figure 92**). If the dimension is 1.484 in. (37.680mm) or greater it must be replaced.

13. Clean all parts again in solvent and thoroughly dry. Coat the new oil seal (6) with fresh fork oil.

14. Install the 2 springs (12) and spring joint piece (13).

15. Install the fork tube assembly into the fork slider and install the oil seal with special tools (**Figure 93**). Take care not to damage the oil seal during installation.

NOTE
These special tools can be improvised. Start the oil seal in by hand, then lay a large washer over it. Drive the seal in with a piece of pipe, which can slide over the fork tube. Make sure the pipe does not mar the fork tube during this procedure. Wrap the fork tube with duct tape to protect it. Make sure the seal is completely seated.

16. Install the internal 48mm circlip (**Figure 95**).

17. Install the fork dust seal (3).

18. Temporarily install the fork top cap (1) until the fork is reinstalled and refilled with fork oil.

FRONT FORK (FREE VALVE TYPE)

Disassembly/Inspection/Assembly

Refer to **Figure 97** for this procedure.

1. Remove the fork top bolt (**Figure 98**).

2. Remove the rubber dust cover (**Figure 99**).

3. Remove the internal 48mm circlip with circlip pliers (**Figure 100**).

4. Place the slider in a vise with soft jaws and remove the Allen bolt (**Figure 101**).

5. Remove the seal retainer and gently pry out the oil seal (**Figure 102**) from the slider.

6. Clean all parts in solvent and thoroughly dry.

7. Check the fork tube for signs of wear or galling.

8. Check the lower slider for dents or exterior damage that may cause the upper fork tube to hang up during riding conditions.

9. Inspect the fork spring for wear or distortion; replace if necessary.

10. Clean all parts again in solvent and thoroughly dry. Coat the new oil seal with fresh fork oil.

11. Install a new oil seal in the slider with a suitable size socket (**Figure 103**).

12. Install the fork tube assembly into the fork slider and install the internal circlip (**Figure 104**).

13. Apply Loctite Lock'N'Seal to the threads of the Allen bolt and install it. Tighten it securely.

REAR SUSPENSION

Major rear suspension components are 2 shock absorbers, 2 springs, and a swing arm.

Shock Absorbers and Springs

The rear shock absorbers are not serviceable, and must be replaced in the event of malfunction.

1. Remove shock absorber mounting bolts (**Figure 105**) and pull shock absorbers off.

2. Compress the shock absorber with a special spring compressor as shown in **Figure 106**, until the spring seat can be removed. Then release pressure from the tool.

3. To install the new shock absorbers, reverse the preceding steps.

Swing Arm

The pivot section of the swing arm is susceptible to wear, especially in the shaft and

7

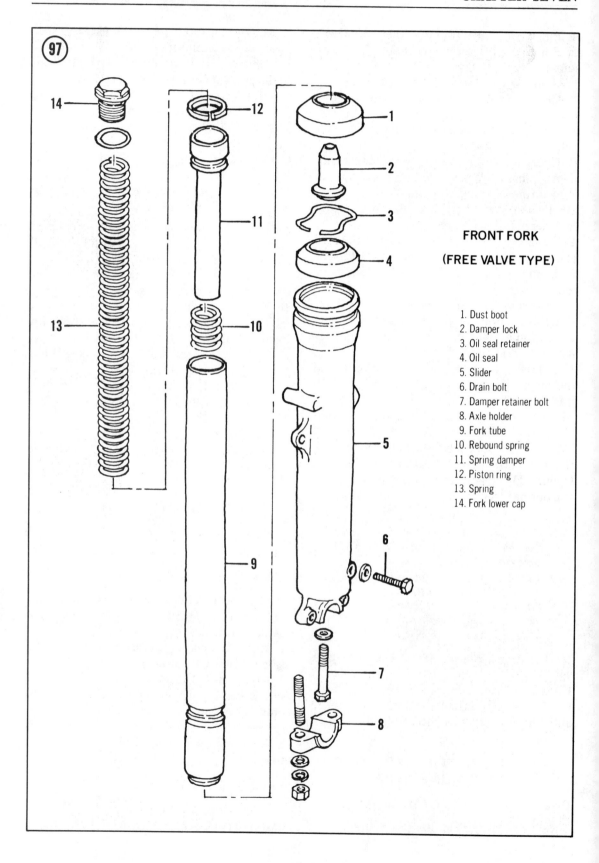

(97)

FRONT FORK

(FREE VALVE TYPE)

1. Dust boot
2. Damper lock
3. Oil seal retainer
4. Oil seal
5. Slider
6. Drain bolt
7. Damper retainer bolt
8. Axle holder
9. Fork tube
10. Rebound spring
11. Spring damper
12. Piston ring
13. Spring
14. Fork lower cap

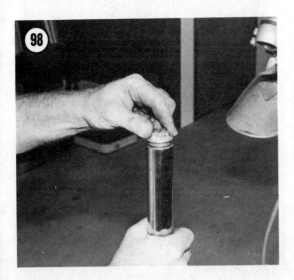

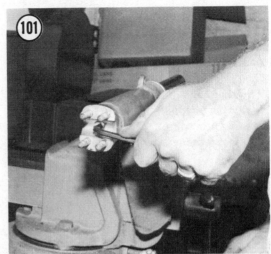

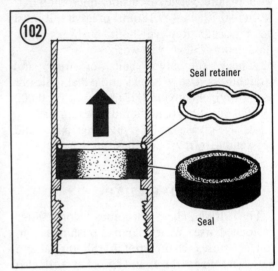

Seal retainer

Seal

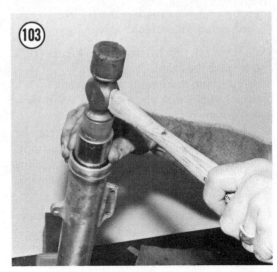

7

bushings. Replace the pivot shaft if it is bent more than 0.02 in. (0.5mm). Replace bushings and/or shaft if the clearance between them exceeds 0.014 in. (0.35mm).

Disassemble the swing arm and grease its pivot shaft and bushings every 6,000 miles (9,000 km). Refer to **Figure 107** for the following procedure:

1. Remove the rear wheel as described in this chapter.
2. Remove the drive chain.
3. Remove the hex nut, washer and dust seal cap.
4. Withdraw the pivot bolt and remove the swing arm from the bike's frame.
5. Measure the inside diameter of the bushing with a bore gauge or inside micrometer. If worn to 0.795 in. (20.18mm) or greater it must be replaced. Replace both bushings even though only one may be worn.
6. Check the pivot bolt for wear and straightness. Use V-blocks and a dial indicator as shown in **Figure 108**. If the runout is 0.002 in. (0.05mm) or greater it must be replaced.
7. Apply grease to all pivoting parts and reassemble by reversing these steps.

DRIVE CHAIN

The drive chain becomes worn after prolonged use. Wear in pins, bushings, and rollers causes chain stretch. Sliding action between roller surfaces and sprocket teeth also contributes to wear.

Cleaning and Adjustment

1. Disconnect the master link (**Figure 109**) and remove the chain.
2. Clean chain thoroughly with solvent.
3. Rinse chain with clean solvent, then blow dry with compressed air.
4. Examine chain carefully for wear or damage. Replace if there is any doubt as to its condition. If chain is OK, lubricate by soaking in oil, or any special chain lubricants available in most motorcycle supply stores.
5. Install the chain. Be sure that the master link is installed as shown in **Figure 109**.
6. Adjust the drive chain and rear brake as described in Chapter Three.

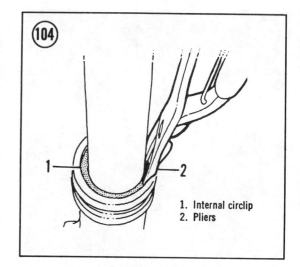

1. Internal circlip
2. Pliers

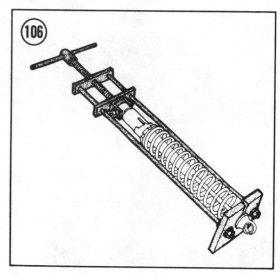

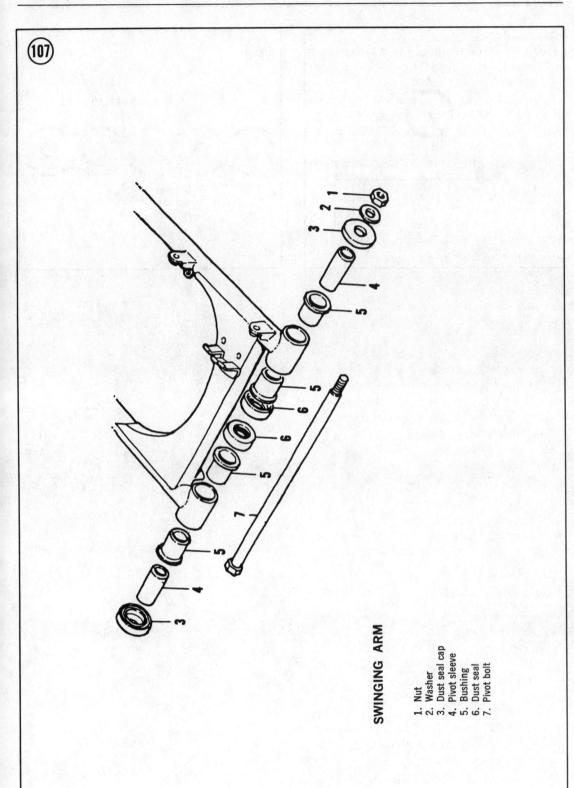

SWINGING ARM

1. Nut
2. Washer
3. Dust seal cap
4. Pivot sleeve
5. Bushing
6. Dust seal
7. Pivot bolt

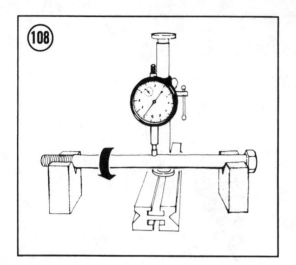

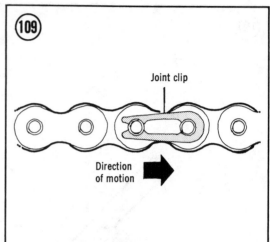

INDEX

8

CB250 – U.K.

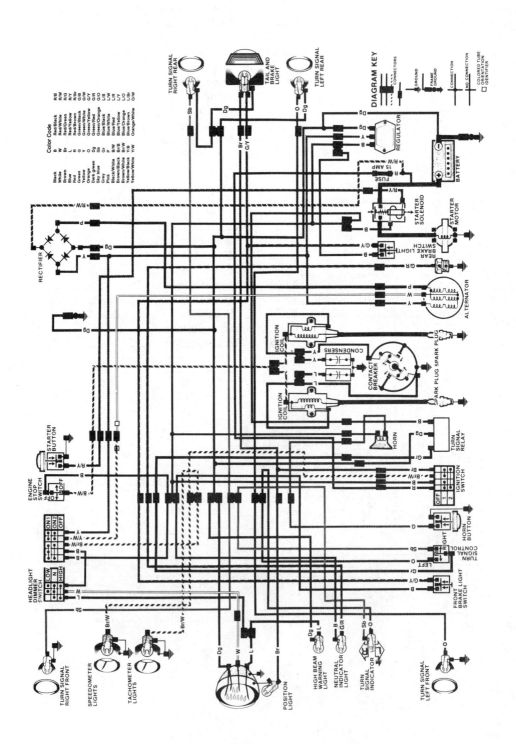

CB & CL350K4 – U.S.

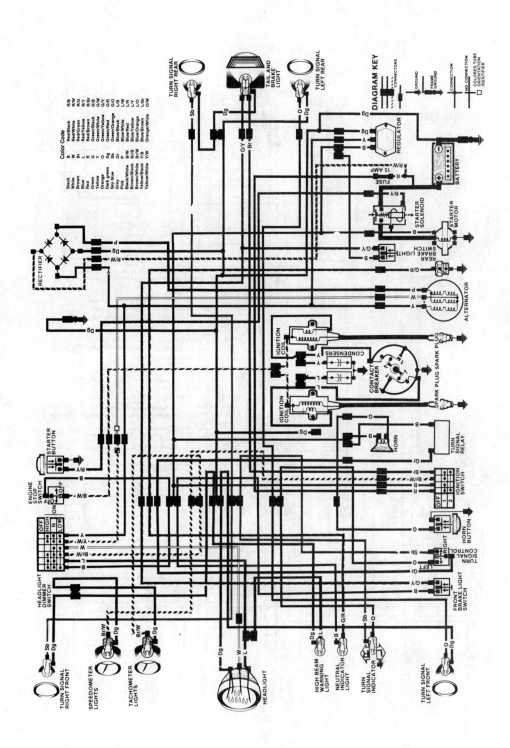

CB & CL350K4 – General Export

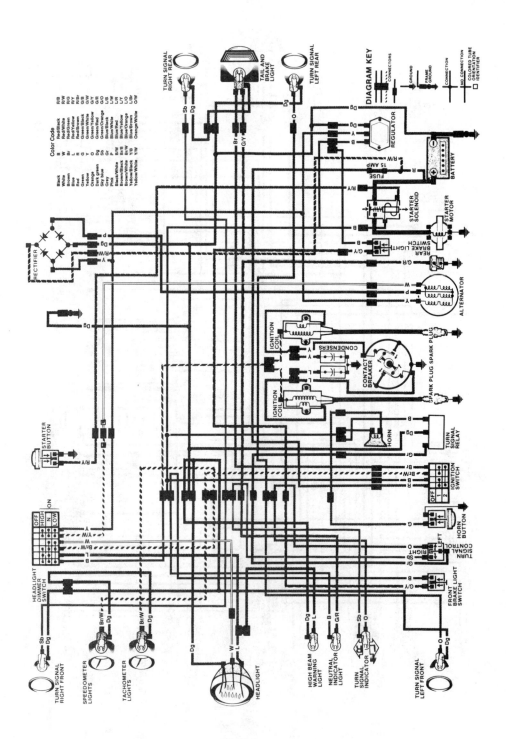

CB350G

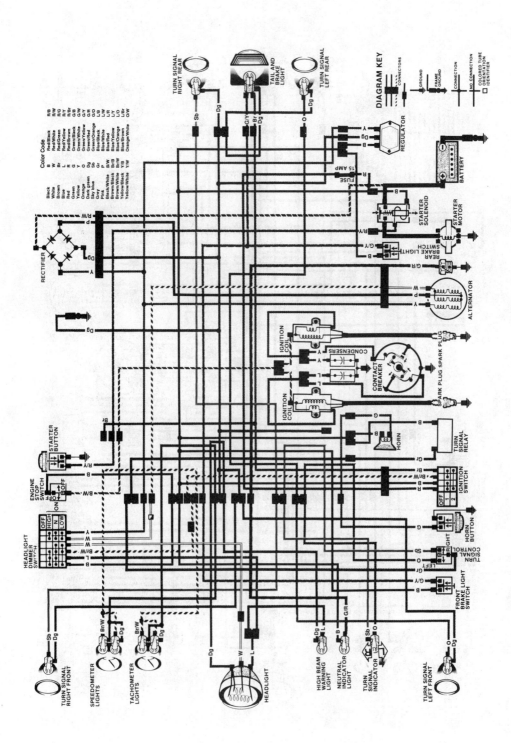

SL350

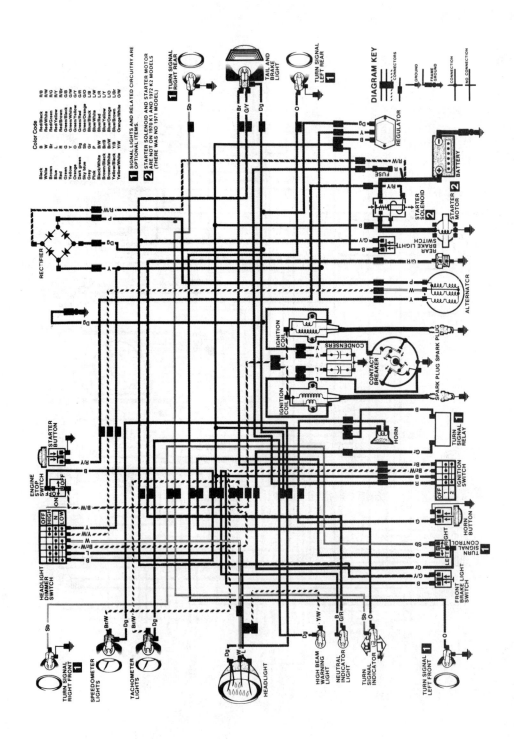

SL350K2 – U.S.

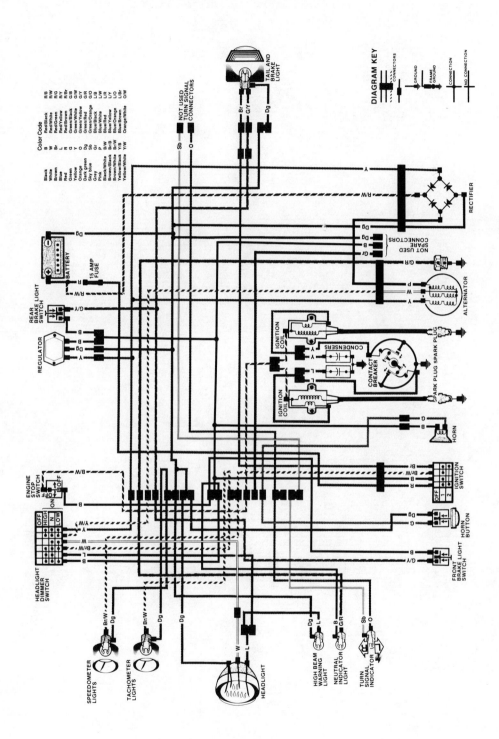

NOTES

NOTES

NOTES

NOTES

NOTES

MAINTENANCE LOG

Service Performed   **Mileage Reading**

Service Performed	Mileage Reading				
Oil change (example)	2,836	5,782	8,601		